Bharatha Natya Yoga

Understanding Bharatha Natyam as an Embodiment of Ashta Anga Yoga

APARNA RAMASWAMY, Ph.D.

BLESSINGS

In the words of the author's *Guru* and *Natya-acharya* **Shri. V.P. Dhananjayan**, Aparna is a "dancer, teacher and communicator par excellence. Her satvika-abhinaya (physical, mental & spiritually involved expressions) combined with flawless language of an erudite scholarship, sets forth a new definition to the concept of Natya as the ultimate Yoga of all senses. As her Guru and mentor, I am very happy and proud that Aparna has found meaning to our teachings beyond our own perceptions.

This is what a true sishya (student) should do".

CONTENTS

TRANSLITERATION AND DEFINITION OF SANSKRIT WORDS

This study transliterates Sanskrit words into English without using diacritical marks to aid pronunciation. Instead, in keeping with arts based research methodology, an auditory guide is provided as an aid in pronunciation of Sanskrit words.

http://www.youtube.com/watch?v=syw-jnS3Xf8&feature=youtu.be

Additionally, since this study suggests transdisciplinary understandings of some of the words, a glossary with a preferred description is not provided. Instead, each concept is described within the text of this study, in specific context. Sanskrit words such as *yogi*, *mudra*, *karana*, etc. are used in the same manner, both in singular and plural sense. The accompanying English phrasing clarifies its use.

Words such as re-vision, re-introduce, re-create, re-emerge, re-experience, etc. are used as hyphenated words to re-iterate the message of this study to re-claim and re-integrate what already exists and to additionally emphasize its essential meaning of re-vision of an ancient dance style. While discussing certain hermeneutic interpretations, I have used language in present tense to reflect and make transparent the subjective and interactive nature of a researcher's critical engagement with the information being gathered from textual material.

Gurubhyo Namaha
Salutations to Guru

Twameva mata cha pita twameva
You are mother and father

Twameva bandhushcha sakha twameva
You are relative and friend

Twameva vidya dravinam twameva
You are knowledge and wealth

Twameva sarvam mama deva deva
You are everything, my Supreme Being

With sincere gratitude to all the teachers who came into my life to guide me. Thank you for all the lessons ~ Aparna

1. NATYA YOGA: INTRODUCTION

In this book, I am exploring the thesis that *Bharatha Natyam* embodies the *ashta anga* principles of yoga wherein the dance form of Bharatha Natyam creates *rasa*, a meditative experience that *yoga* refers to as *dhyana*. *Bharatha Natyam* (also written as *Bharatanatyam*) is a classical dance style from Southern India that is practiced as an interpretive storytelling dance form. It is a present-day descendant of an ancient Indian dramatic dance form called natya, first described in the text of Natyasastra. Whereas, ashta anga are eight principles of yoga, first described by Patanjali in the text of Yogasutra. My inquiry is to link the ashta anga principles of yoga with the practice of Bharatha Natyam, and re-vision it as Natya Yoga. I propose that the language of ashta anga yoga provides clarity in understanding how body movements, feet positions, percussive rhythm, etc. facilitate *rasa,* an inner experience of dance. I propose that *Bharatha Natyam* transforms to *Natya Yoga,* when its focus shifts to the inner experience of dancing. I also suggest that *rasa,* the experience of dancing is an intended outcome of all forms of *natya* as described by Bharatha in his text of *Natyasastra*. And as such, it is important that the essential qualities of *natya* percolate and permeate its descendant dance forms, including *Bharatha Natyam*. In this book, the words dance and Indian dance are used interchangeably with *Bharatha Natyam*, except when I specifically state otherwise. Similarly, since this study utilizes *Bharatha Natyam* to explore its embodiment as *Natya Yoga*, the words *Natya Yoga* also refer to *Bharatha Natya Yoga*. The expression *ashta anga yoga* specifically refers to the *ashta anga* principles of *yoga* and not to any particular practice of yoga.

Bharatha Natyam

Bharatha Natyam is a classical dance style from Southern India, practiced as an interpretive storytelling art form that narrates stories from mythology, religion, history, and romantic poetry. It is percussive with precise feet movements and stamping; fluid in its body movements; vigorous in arm movements; expressive and sophisticated hand gestures; emotional in the dancer's experience of the song; and communicative with facial expressions. The dancer dances in synchrony with the rhythm of music, and experiences the *bhava* (emotions) of the lyrics that are sung in varying melodic patterns. The dancer utilizes *mudra* (hand gestures) and *abhinaya* (expression) to convey this emotional experience to the audience. The nonverbal interactions between dancer, musician, and audience enhance the integrated experience of dancing, music, and its expression. This collaborative creation of the dancing experience, called *rasa* is the purpose of dramatic dance - *natya* (Vatsyayan, 1968). In this study, Bharatha Natyam is representative of its ancestral, yet extant form of *natya*.

Natyasastra, a treatise on Indian dramaturgy by sage Bharatha, described the import of creating this emotional experience, especially for the audience. The overarching goal of Indian dance and drama (*natya)* was the experience of emotion in music wherein a dancer's body became a vehicle to experience and convey the emotion to the audience (Rangacharya, 1986). However, the *Natyasastra* did not offer language to describe this process in dance or the significance of evoking *rasa* in the audience.

Yoga

Yoga is a term that describes practices by which the human body and mind are harmonized with the universal source of energy, which pervades on the outside. *Yoga* also refers to the communion of internal and external energies. The earliest text that spoke of *yoga* was the *Yogasutra* written several hundreds of years ago by Patanjali. The *Yogasutra* outlined essential principles (*ashta anga*) that facilitated this connection but did not prescribe any specific practice of these eight, *ashta anga* principles. The *ashta anga* described eight principles that led to a union (*samadhi*) of human self with a metaphysical universal being (*Ishvara*). The eighth *anga - samadhi* led to such a transcendence of the physical self. Since the *Yogasutra* was written, there have been several additions, revisions, and interpretations of *ashta anga yoga* especially with regards to their practice. In today's world, the word *yoga* is most commonly associated with *hata yoga* and physical postures, or *asana* that is only one among eight of the *ashta anga*.

Objectives and Overview

The word *yoga* refers both to the practice and its resulting experience of *samadhi*. Some forms of yoga seem to emphasize the aspect of self-transcendence in their practices while others work towards the goal of union (*samadhi*), the eighth limb of *ashta anga*. This study explores the form of *Bharatha Natyam* as related to the *ashta anga* principles of yoga leading to the dancer's experience of dance and its comparability to the meditative experience of yoga. There are five stated research objectives that serve to establish the context of this study on *Natya Yoga,* and ground the form and experience of *Bharatha Natyam* as appropriate to its suggested practice of *ashta anga* principles of yoga.

3

Chapters 2 and 3 review literature that establishes history and context of this study. Chapter 2 explores the practice of *Bharatha Natyam* tracing its evolution over recent times establishing its link to the form of *natya* that is described in *Natyasastra*. Since my inquiry is to link the principles of *ashta anga yoga* with the practice of *Bharatha Natyam*, the focus in Chapter 3 is on yoga practices that work towards union (*samadhi*) through physical and mental observances as described in *ashta anga yoga*. Chapter 3 discusses how various schools of yoga practice a*shta anga yoga* principles and the differences in their approach, with a view to establish a base for this study's interpretation of *Bharatha Natyam* as a practice of a*shta anga yoga*.

Research Objective 1: Describe The Inner Experience of Dancing *Bharatha Natyam*

Method: Narrative, Heuristic and Arts Based Research

My study is to liken the practice of *Bharatha Natyam* to yoga that is based on *ashta anga*. In this context, the experience of dancing is discussed as comparable to the meditative experience of yoga. Describing the inner experience of dancing is an appropriate first objective as it establishes a frame of reference for the experience of dance that this study further delves into. Additionally, this is an unique contribution to the existing literature on practice of dance, especially *Bharatha Natyam*. Presently, literature on experience of Indian dancing emphasizes the concept of *rasa*—experience of dance—often from the audience perspective. The dancer's experience of dancing is minimally represented, especially in Indian dance.

Discussing their dancing experiences Marian Chace, Mary Whitehouse, Joan Chodorow, and Anna Halprin have written about their dancing as a dancer's integrated expression of feeling one with movement (Levy, 1992). Dancers discussing their experience of dance have referred to a feeling of "being danced" while using their body as a "vehicle" of expression in "authentic movement" (Levy, 1992). *Natya,* while privileging extensive and elaborate rhythmic and fluid body movements is distinctive in its emphasis on a dancer's emotional experience and expression of the lyrical content of the song and dance. However, there is scant literature on a dancer's experience of emotional resonance with *natya*. While the *Natyasastra* described how the dancer's body is used to create *rasa*, there is very little said about its relevance, and even less about its experience. In my reading of several other texts on Indian dancing, I found that the dancer's experience—dancer's *rasa*—is not represented.

To address this gap in literature, Chapter 4 aims to develop a narrative and a video documentation of my experience of dancing *Bharatha Natyam*. It describes the dancing experience—*rasa* in *Bharatha Natyam*. The narrative provides the context and range of experience in dance—over a dancer's lifetime chronicling the developmental nature of dancing experience. The narrative also journeys into the changing nature of experience responsive to venues, dancing partners, specific dances, and other situational factors. The narrative describes the experience of pure movements, called *nritta*; experience of expressive dance, *nritya*; and its emotional experience—*rasa*. Chapter 4 languages the experience of dancing with rhythm and melody, while performing for others and its experience when dancing is a private practice for self. The narrative proposes language to describe my experience while dancing in synchrony with music and sensing the integrated harmony in my body. Chapter 4 describes the interiority of my experience as I resonate with the emotion and rhythm of music.

The descriptive narrative provides a broader canvas for describing the experience of dancing that is delved into with further depth in the video recording of my dance. Sharing and inviting viewers to experience my dancing, I have created several segments that share different dance sequences. These sequences convey the range of a *Bharatha Natyam* repertoire and provide a visual representation of the narrative, at a specific moment in time and space. Each sequence is preceded by an introductory description of the context of that particular dance in the repertoire and the dance is followed by a heuristic exploration of my

5

experience while dancing for this specific recording. The narrative provides a range of my dancing *rasa* over my lifetime and the arts based heuristic video brings out with further depth my *rasa* specific to each dance recorded for the purpose of this study.

Chapter 7 explores the phenomenological aspects of dancing with special focus dedicated to the form of *Bharatha Natyam* that evokes the experience, termed *rasa*. Chapter 8 delves with further depth into the interiority of the experience of dancing from a dancer's introspective perspective. This aspect of exploring an experience in self teases out the intricacies and complexities of my dancing experience. While the entire process of immersion, introspection, analysis, and synthesis is representative of a heuristic method, Chapters 7 and 8 describe in detail this heuristic process of understanding the phenomenon of dancing.

Research Objective #2: Understanding The Message In Natyasastra—Rasa Is The Purpose of Natya

Method: Hermeneutic Research

While dancing evokes *rasa* that is personal and unique to me, it is also important to note that the premise of all classical Indian dances (descendants of *natya*) is to evoke *rasa*. Experience of *rasa* while individually textured is not an unintended outcome of dancing. In fact, review of the *Natyasastra* suggests that a primary purpose of *natya* is to evoke *rasa* and a dancer is instructed on utilizing body movements and emotional expression in order to evoke *rasa*. It is important for this study to establish that the premise of *Bharatha Natyam* (this study's representative of *natya)* is to create *rasa* and establish that it is an intended outcome, with a textured experience that is unique to each dancer and dance.

Natyasastra has described specific emotional states (*bhava*) that the dancer steps into, while dancing. It provides detailed instructions on how the face should appear, how the body should be postured, etc. in order to create the emotion in the dancer. It has explained how this emotional experience is expressed appropriately so that it can be communicated to the audience, who can then share the experience of the dancer. It has described body movements, the emotionality conveyed by the position and turns of the body, specified hand gestures that express particular emotions, described how the eyes glances express mood, etc. While the *Natyasastra* has suggested, implied, and reiterated that *natya* is intended for creation of *rasa*, this aspect has become less represented in its practice, especially with regards to *Bharatha Natyam*.

It is reasonable to assume that dance as a practice existed before the *Natyasastra* was written as a way to describe and codify its form. It is also reasonable to note the sophistication of its practice as indicated by the depth of its documentation in *Natyasastra*. It invites the suggestion that perhaps there was a subtler and under represented aspect of this dancing—which extended well beyond the interpretive storytelling aspects. This study explores one such aspect—the meditative experience that transcends the physical form of *Bharatha Natyam*. The hermeneutic interpretations of the *Yogasutra* suggest a language that may provide an understanding for this aspect of dancing. Chapter 6 is dedicated to the interpretations on the form and experience of *ashta anga yoga*.

Chapter 5 introduces the *Natyasastra* and explores the explicit and implicit purpose of *natya*—the path of *natya* (*nritta, nritya, bhava* and *abhinaya*) leading to the experience of *rasa*. The texts used are translations and commentaries on *Natyasastra*, translations of *Abhinaya Darpana* (a text dedicated to dance aspects of *Natyasastra*), and other texts discussing *rasa* and aesthetic experience. The *Natyasastra* has three areas of description—architecture and physical surroundings of dance hall; expressive dance techniques, and musical depiction of rhythm and melody. The role of rhythm and melody in music that enhanced the experience of dance is discussed. The element of pure movement, *nritta* is described along with the significance of cadence of movements, *karana*, which are described in great detail in *Natyasastra*. The relevance of specific feet positions, postures, and artistic hand gestures (*nritta mudra*) is explored. The role of expressive hand gestures along with facial expressions is discussed with regards to expression (*abhinaya*) of emotions (*bhava*). Several emotions are described in *Natyasastra* as specific personality traits of a character (*ashta nayika*) and emotional moods that are depicted (*nava rasa*). The emphasis placed on evoking *rasa* in dancer and audience is reiterated throughout the *Natyasastra*—this is a thread that is woven throughout the discussions in Chapter 5.

Research Objective #3: Discuss How *Bharatha Natyam* Embodies Principles of *Ashta Anga Yoga*

Method: Phenomenological, Heuristic and Hermeneutic Research

Bharatha Natyam as an embodiment of *ashta anga yoga* is a core aspect of this study. In order to discuss this, it is necessary to describe the eight (*ashta*) principles of yoga as first described in *Yogasutra* by sage Patanjali. Several interpretations and commentaries are included in this discussion of *ashta anga yoga*. Chapter 6 describes the various interpretations of *ashta anga yoga* while Chapters 7 and 8 discuss how *Bharatha Natyam* is an embodiment of these eight principles. Chapter 6 is a study of hermeneutic interpretations of the *Yogasutra* while Chapter 7 undertakes the phenomenological study of *rasa* that is evoked by the form and practice of *Bharatha Natyam*. Chapter 8 delves in greater depth into the experience of *rasa* following a heuristic method.

In today's world, the word *yoga* is most commonly associated with physical postures, or *asana*. This is an aspect of yoga, popularized by *Hata Yoga* (Ramacharaka, 1930). Similarly, there are other approaches, such as *Bhakti Yoga* (defined as yoga of devotion), *Karma Yoga* (yoga of selfless service), and *Jnana Yoga* (yoga of knowledge) (Narayanan, 2009, p. 7). A later approach that brings several practices together has been termed Integral Yoga that emphasizes yoga's central purpose of mind, body, and spirit connection (Chaudhuri, 1965).

In Chapter 6, discussion is focused on practices of *ashta anga* principles of yoga that lead to union (*samadhi*). Hermeneutic interpretations of *Yogasutra* by various authors are considered along with practice-oriented understanding of *ashta anga yoga* by various schools of yoga. Chapter 6 further delineates each principle of *ashta anga yoga* outlined in Chapter 3, incorporating interpretations by authors such as Feuerstein, Whicher, Swami Sivananda, Swami Rama, Kripalvananda, Iyengar, and Swami Satchidananda.

Chapter 7 reintroduces the arts based engagement shared in Chapter 4 and discusses the form of *Bharatha Natyam* as an embodiment of *ashta anga yoga*. The external practices of *yama, niyama, asana, pranayama* are discussed in their integrated form of *Bharatha Natyam* while *pratyahara* and *dharana* are described as straddling the external form and internal experience of *Bharatha Natyam*. This chapter is dedicated to re-visioning the form of *Bharatha Natyam* as an integrated practice of the eight (*ashta anga*) principles of yoga. The purely internal experience of *dhyana* and *samadhi* are discussed in a separate chapter in the context of how *rasa,* the dancing experience of *Bharatha Natyam* compares to meditative immersion in yoga.

Research Objective #4: Bridging *Natya Yoga* and *Ashta Anga Yoga*: Experience of *Rasa* and S*amadhi*

Method Proposed: Heuristic, Hermeneutic, and Arts Based Research

Authors such as Abhinavagupta and Vatsyayan have discussed how *rasa* relates to *samadhi*. *Rasa* has been compared to the mystical union in *samadhi* and since *natya* evokes rasa, *natya* is suggested to be a practice of *yoga* that leads to oneness. Building further on this suggestion, this present study discusses in depth the experience of *rasa* and its comparability to *dhyana* and *samadhi*, the seventh and eighth concepts in *ashta anga yoga*. Chapter 8 is dedicated to describing *rasa* and its similarity to meditative immersion in *dhyana* and *samadhi*. Additionally, an arts based video recording of a specially choreographed dance is shared to invite viewers to experience this meditative immersion in dance. The discussion on my experience of dancing is explored as a heuristic inquiry, seeking to know the nuanced experience of my immersion in dancing and a co-existing awareness of this immersion. Hermeneutic interpretations of *samadhi* are discussed to highlight a comparable experience in yoga practices—the quality of meditative immersion and awareness of this immersion.

Samadhi, an experience of self, leading to its transcendence is an objective of *ashta anga yoga*. Practices that create a self-transcending experience are practices of yoga. For instance, fulfilling cosmic work with selfless action is the essence of *Karma Yoga*; dedicated and devoted surrender to God is a practice of *Bhakti Yoga*. The experience of self in relation to the universe is the goal of yoga—to unite self with the universal spirit—to create oneness.

Rasa, an experience of dancing is the essence of Indian dance (Vatsyayan, 1968). Stylized and percussive body movements, expressive hand gestures, and facial expressions convey the emotional experience and make it overt through the act of dancing. Expressions of such experiences often act as a recursive loop in enhancing the experience not only for the dancer but also for the audience. This experience, *rasa*, transcends dancer, audience, musician, dance, and music—it is all of it (Vatsyayan, 1968).

While these experiences may have been studied and described independently, there has not been adequate work done to bring them together. My objective is to inquire into the experiences of *rasa* and *samadhi* with a view to bridge the missing link between *Bharatha Natyam* and *ashta anga yoga*.

Research Objective #5: Re-Vision of *Bharatha Natya*m as *Natya Yoga*

This study suggests that when *Bharatha Natyam* is practiced with awareness of its embodiment of *ashta anga yoga*, it is a revision of *Bharatha Natyam* as *Natya Yoga*—a practice of *ashta anga yoga*. Historically, Indian dance has reflected changing societal and historical factors by responding with adaptations in its form and practices. While several distinct styles of Indian dancing have emerged, there are shared commonalities amongst them. However, over time, the common element of expression of emotional experience may have become overshadowed by emphasis on movement and rhythm. While this study focuses on *Bharatha Natyam*, the suggestion is that the essence of *natya* is *rasa* and an integral shared aspects in classical Indian dance forms.

Chapter 8 seeks to emphasize the significance of the experience of dancing, *rasa* and suggests that meditative focus on evoking and experiencing *rasa* transforms *Bharatha Natyam* into *Natya yoga*. While my study speaks directly to *Bharatha Natyam*, the principles have the potential to be extrapolated to other creative practices of yoga.

Methodology

I began this study to find a language that helped me understand the experience of dancing *Bharatha Natyam*. While seeking an understanding that fit my experience I stumbled upon *ashta anga* principles in the *Yogasutra*. Upon finding this language that resonated with my experience of dancing I was compelled to study how *Bharatha Natyam* embodied these eight principles—both in its form and its experience. The purpose of my quest was twofold—to describe the experience of *rasa* and to inquire into explanations for this phenomenon. In order to adequately represent the form of *Bharatha Natyam* that evokes the experience of *rasa* it is important to lay the appropriate foundation for this study.

The phenomenon of dancing experience has been referred to as *rasa*. However the description of its experience has not been adequately represented in dancing literature. In order for me to seek a language that resonates with my experience, it would be critical to describe this experience multi-dimensionally. The phenomenology of dancing includes several aspects such as its form of practice and its experience. The experience of dancing can be described specific to a particular dance or a specified time or location. The range of experiences varies over time and influenced by environmental and developmental factors. In order to represent each of these aspects adequately, I use an integrative methodology that incorporates multiple qualitative methods.

I use a narrative methodology to describe the range of my dancing experiences over my lifetime. I also share several video recordings to invite viewers to step into the experiential world that arts based research makes possible. I expand on the hermeneutic language that *Natyasastra* provides to describe the form and experience of *natya*. In my study of *Yogasutra* I delve into hermeneutic interpretations by other scholars on their understanding and practice of *ashta anga yoga*. When correlating the form and experience of dance with the interpretations of *ashta anga* the study is consistent with a phenomenological approach in understanding the experience of dancing. While recording, the experience of each dance varies and in order to delve further into each experiential state, I chose a heuristic method. A heuristic method of self-inquiry affords me the ability to introspect, analyze, and re-experience the immersed absorption while dancing. These multiple methods help convey the multi-dimensional quality of dancing experience and suggest a new language to conceptualize this experience.

Qualitative Method

A study dictates the choice of methodology that best suited its stated objectives. In particular, this study emphasizes the qualitative aspect of dance and of yoga practice. For this reason, a qualitative research methodology is an appropriate choice. With this or another similar study in place, a researcher interested in verifying the efficacy of *Natya Yoga* or other yoga practices may choose to employ quantitative research through assessments and quantitative measurements of the change due to such practices. For the purpose of this study, in order to explore and better language the experience of dance a qualitative approach is an appropriate choice.

Giorgi distinguished natural science research as that which creates quantitative measures whereas the alternative human science methods stress the qualitative dimension of the outcome (Kruger, 1983, p. 21). Giorgi described that natural science research methods measure and analyze data into components, while human science methods arrive at meanings, seeking to describe rather than define. In natural science methods, the emphasis is on determining links between clearly identified variables, using experiments that are ostensibly repeatable. By contrast, in human science methods, the premise and emphasis is that the phenomenon being studied is not one-dimensional but can "be known only through its varied manifestations" (Kruger, 1983, p. 21). In natural science research, the role of the researcher is as an independent observer, while in human science research the recognition is that all observation is made possible with a participative engagement of the researcher. Human science research recognizes, facilitates, and reclaims the role of the subjectivity for the researcher and the "intersection of researcher and research" (Kruger, 1983, p. 21). The unique contribution of the subjective eye that views the data is included as an important factor in human science research studies.

A scientific community member may consider scientific research as the norm that yields "incontrovertible facts" (Giorgi, 1985, p. vii). These facts imply validity based on their comparison with a "pre-established and objective (consensually agreed on) criterion" (Eckartsberg, 1983, p. 199). Therefore when branches of science follow quantitative methods of natural science research, they have only "partial success" in studying the shifting complexity of human phenomena (Giorgi, 1985, p. vii). As a protest against "scientific and positivistic bias in psychology," the field of human science research arose to reclaim the "structural face validity of personal experiences" (Eckartsberg, 1983, pp. 199–200). The unique contribution of varying personal experiences and perspectives were reclaimed for their validity in research studies.

Phenomenological Research

This study revolves around a dancer's experience of dancing. The experience is influenced by several internal and external factors such as the form of *Bharatha Natyam*, the physical venue, the quality of music and musical accompaniment, the choice of dances, the emotional state of the dancer, etc. In order to explore the various interrelated factors that create and affect the experience of dancing, a phenomenological study of this experience is an appropriate approach.

Studies on the human phenomena—phenomenological studies, build on Kierkegaard's philosophy of the "unique and unrepeatable" nature of man's existence and experiences (Kruger, 1983, p. 17). The emphasis was not on creating an absolute or irrefutable validation or support of a hypothesis. Instead, the focus was on understanding the "lived and experienced" human phenomenon and emphasized the "complexities and richness" of human reality (Giorgi, 1985, pp. vii–viii). While this methodology has no quantitative measurement, its strength is to "show qualitative differences" (Giorgi, 1985, p. 6). It is a "visionary" discipline rather than an exact "measurement" science (Eckartsberg, 1983, p. 200).

A phenomenological study is one that is "grounded in actual human experience" (Mruk, 1983, p. 141). Husserl, Merleau-Ponty, Sartre, Heidegger, Marcel, and Ricoeur were some of the philosophers and contributors to phenomenological research. The Duquesne School and in particular, researchers such as Giorgi and Maes pioneered a phenomenological approach to research with a view to understand the qualitative complexity and richness of human experiences.

Narrative Research

Phenomenology is the study of lived experience. In this study, the focus is on the experience of dancing *Bharatha Natyam*. As a starting point, it is important to have a working description of the inner experience of dancing *Bharatha Natyam*, which is also my first research objective. In Indian dance literature, there are hermeneutic interpretations on various aspects of dance techniques. Recently, dancers of various classical Indian dances are discovering and reclaiming commonalities in their distinctly stylized dance forms. However, there is minimal writing on *rasa,* especially as a dancing experience from the perspective of a dancer. A simple explanation is that it may have been uncommon for dancers to also be scholarly writers and therefore scholars wrote about the experience of dancing, with an outsider's perspective. Another suggestion may be that such experiences are hard to describe with words, in a way that does justice to its richness. A narrative that seeks to describe the range of experiences in dancing not only serves the purpose of this study, but also addresses a gap in Indian dance literature. As a literary contribution, this narrative will explore the use of descriptive words and suggest a vocabulary to express the interiority of the dancing experience.

Narratives can be any "spoken or written presentation"; narratives can be writing that describes a "sequence of events arranged in temporal order"; a narrative can also be a specifically designed interview to "elicit a particular kind of data" (Schwandt, 2007, p. 201). Narratives are a "context-rich mode" of expression that can include "spatial and temporal ordering of experience" (Deslauriers, 1992, p. 187). Narratives explore the "breadth and plurality" of a theme or experience with a "depth and intensity" of approach (Braud, 1998).

Often narratives can provide a wide range of experiences drawn from different respondents discussing varying aspects of their experience over time and space. As a tool of analysis, narrative research facilitates making meaning of the various 'stories' that are narrated (Schwandt, 2007, p. 203). The emerging or recurrent theme can be identified and distilled as appropriate to the study. This concept of finding meaning or a larger story that holds the individual narratives is seen frequently in narrative studies. This aspect of an "analytic stance" in developing a "defensive interpretive framework" is less represented in this study (Wells, 2011, p. 43). The narrative serves to position me as I enter this study as a dancer with a lifelong engagement and experience of dancing. The narrative provides a rich text of experiences that are over time in different physical settings. The "thematic content" and "concept" of narratives is used in creating the story of my dancing experiences over the past 30 years (Riessman, 2008).

In this study, the narrative is drawn from my own life experiences as a dancer. The narrative describes my experiences of dance over time and in different physical spaces over my developmental and adult years. The narrative describes my bank of dancing experience collected from years of dancing as a solo, duo and group performer. The narrative also pulls in my experience of dancing not as a public performance, but one for private enjoyment. In essence, this narrative approach conveys a wide spectrum of my dancing experiences that describes the multi-dimensionality of *Bharatha Natyam*.

The narrative research invites an exploration into various aspects of my experience while dancing and provides an expansive spectrum of my experiences. It introduces my perspective as I enter the study to understand the nuances of my experience, while simultaneously searching for a language that fits my experiences. With a frame of reference that this study aims to provide, further narratives may be sought from other dancers to explore how others experience dancing.

The limitation of a multi-dimensional description of experience of dance can be a limited focus on the depth of any one experience, specific to time and space. In this study, this aspect is countered by incorporating other methods such as arts based and heuristic inquiry that help develop more focus on specific nuances of my experience of dancing.

Arts Based Research

Dance itself is an expression of an experience. Any attempt to translate this experience in words can dilute this expression even when done with care. It would be ideal if the viewer could experience *rasa* and have a deeper knowing of it. An arts based approach carries the promise to recreate some aspects of the experience for the observer. Barone and Eisner consider arts based research as "an effort to extend beyond the limiting constraints of discursive communication in order to express meanings that otherwise would be ineffable" (2012, p. 1). In some ways, arts based approach is a heuristic research "through which we deepen" and expand our understandings (Barone & Eisner, 2012, p. 3).

Leavy wrote "I think what the arts most offer and what traditional academic writing most fails to accomplish is *resonance*" (2009, p. ix). Dance combines elements of several art forms—it is "musical, performative, visual, poetic, autobiographical, and can serve narrative" (Leavy, 2009, p. 179). The experience of dancing belongs entirely to the moment, existing only in performance and is hard to completely capture with descriptions. I offer a video documentary of my dancing as an expression of my emotional experience, *rasa*, in *Bharatha Natyam*.

The video documentation is designed to re-create for the viewer the unfolding of a traditional repertoire in a *Bharatha Natyam* performance. Seven dances are shared and each dance is preceded and followed by extempore speaking. The introduction to each dance provides its context in the repertoire, describes the interpretive relevance, and suggests its place in the larger story of the entire performing/viewing experience. Short segments of the dance sequences demonstrate the words that describe the dance, and invite the viewer to experience and understand the dance differently. The symbolism of the dance, the nuances of the dancer's expression, attention to the dancer's experience, and their own response to this provide an opportunity for this different and new understanding.

Each dance is immediately followed by an unscripted and unedited spontaneous introspection on the experience of dancing at that particular time and context of the recording. The viewer hears my experience of dancing, has the awareness of how this was manifested in the dance, knows their own response to the dance, and has the opportunity to integrate the various expressions of my experience of dancing. The viewer's understanding of experience of dancing is further deepened by their direct and intimate experience of dancing. One selected dance is shared in its entirety to invite the viewer to taste the immersive experience of dance. This aspect of immersion and awareness of immersion also sets the foundation for later phenomenological and heuristic discussions of the experience of dancing, *rasa*.

A second shorter documentary is presented to explore how *rasa* relates to *samadhi*. This is shared later, in Chapter 7. My engagement in dance is representative of the research aspect of arts based work, and distinctly different from its use as an expressive tool to convey findings. As I dance, emotions, understandings and insights emerge from my engagement in the experience of dancing. *Bharatha Natyam* is an expression of such an experience that manifests as movement and facial expression.

The songs used in the first set of dances were recorded over twenty years ago and where possible, musical credits have been indicated in the video documentation. For the second dance of *rasa* and *samadhi*, music was specifically commissioned under my direction and specifications, for the primary purpose of this research study. The copyright for this music was obtained from each participating musician.

The narrative introduces me as a dancer with a lifetime of varied experiences in dancing. An arts based approach adds the personal dimension and shares specific dances recorded for this study. In addition to providing a range of experiences, a more focused set of experiences is also provided. Even with this level of sharing, it is critical to contextualize the performance by providing "accompanying textual component" of the representation (Leavy, 2009, p. 180). The heuristic immersion, introspection and synthesis of my experience of dancing serves to provide this context.

Heuristic Research

The root meaning of *heuristic* is from a Greek word *heuriskein* that means "to discover" or "to find" (Moustakas, 1990, p. 9). It is understood to be a practice and process to self-discovery, keeping relevance to that individual's lived experience. A researcher who chooses a heuristic approach undertakes to immerse completely in their experience and bring to conscious awareness all that lies in their tacit knowing. Unlike phenomenology, heuristic study implies that the researcher has "direct, personal" engagement with the studied experience in a "vital, intense and full way" (Moustakas, 1990, p. 14). While phenomenology studies the "essence of the experience," heuristics strives to retain the "essence of the person" who is engaged in the experience (Moustakas, 1990, p. 39). Heuristic research seeks to "reveal" more completely the true meanings of a "phenomenon" of human experience (Moustakas, 1990, p. 42).

The six distinct phases of heuristic research are described as an initial engagement with the experience studied, an immersion into the topic, incubation of inner knowing, illumination of new awareness, explication of emerging meanings and creative synthesis of the understanding (Moustakas, 1990, pp. 27–29). Researchers who claim to follow heuristic research often fail to follow the six steps (Sela-Smith, 2002, p. 70). She identifies these six key components that are intrinsic to heuristic research, including an interactive and engaged dialogue with self that is evidenced as transformational for both the researcher and the reviewer (Sela-Smith, 2002, p. 69). I propose to use a heuristic approach to inquire about my inner experience of *Bharatha Natyam*.

I have come to this stage in my study after intense engagement, immersion and incubation of understanding my experience of dancing. The journey to make overt, my tacit knowing has involved introspection, explication and creative synthesis of the entirety of my experience and understandings. I have been engaged with dance since the age of five years. Despite being an occasionally reluctant student of dance, I persevered in learning, performing and staying engaged with dancing. As a teenager and young adult I was immersed in the performing experience of dance. Upon moving to the United States, I became immersed in the other side of learning—the teaching experience of dance. As I soaked in the experiences, my inner knowing of *rasa* expanded. It was while trying to describe it and teach it to students that I realized my impoverished vocabulary for this task. This set me on my present path to find a language that has helped me better understand my experience of dancing. As I became more aware of my journey, new understandings found me. I resonated with the *ashta anga yoga principles* that I introspect on further. Once I was able to language this new knowing in my own mind, the journey to present it creatively as an integrative synthesis has brought me to this present study. This study that incorporates multiple aspects of presentation is a creative synthesis of my new understanding of how *natya* (and *Bharatha Natyam*) relate to *yoga*.

My heuristic synthesis allows me to voice my experience of movement and an integrated sense of harmony within myself. This will also invite articulation of the intense focus while dancing that coexists with an awareness of physical surroundings including audience engagement. It will allow me to describe multiple levels of awareness even while engaged in the dancing experience. While the new understanding builds on experiential knowing, the language that suggests a different understanding was resourced from texts on *natya* and *yoga*. The contribution and enrichment provided by textual interpretations is best highlighted in using a hermeneutic approach.

Hermeneutic Research

Hermeneutics refers to "the art, theory, and philosophy of interpreting the meaning of an object (a text, work of art, social action, the utterances of another speaker, etc.)" (Schwandt, 2007, p. 136). "Hermeneutic science involves the art of reading a text so that the intention and meaning behind appearances are fully understood" (Moustakas, 1994, p. 9). It suggests iterative understanding that integrates individual parts into a whole, so that understanding is not fragmented but more consistent with the entire message of the text. The individual as an interpreter seeks to understand the essence of what is viewed using his pre-understandings gained from previous experience and knowledge. When the interpretation does not make sense or is ineffective, then the interpreter has the option of reviewing the source (textual or non-textual) to come up with a new understanding. This process of recognition and interpretation is referred to as a hermeneutic circle (Schwandt, 2007, p. 134). The interpretive stance may be objective (exegetical) or creative (isogetical) and the interpreted material may be textual (within text) or non-textual.

Like heuristics, hermeneutic research focuses on the wholeness of experience and searches for meanings rather than explanations of the experience (Moustakas, 1994, p. 21). However, in hermeneutic phenomenology, the interpretation is in service of explaining the phenomenon of the experience and the highlighting factors that may be taken for granted (Laverty, 2003, p. 7). In the context of this study, my experience of dancing may be a personal and unintended outcome of my dancing. However, the text of *Natyasastra* and commentaries on it clearly indicate that the premise of *natya* is to evoke *rasa*. This aspect of *natya* bears reiteration. I propose to use hermeneutic methods to interpret selected sections of *Natyasastra* that relate to the experience of dance. A rough third of the text deals with architectural and structural codification for the physical dancing space. A second third describes in detail specific movements, positions, postures, hand gestures, facial expressions, and even glances of the eyes that help create emotional experiences in the dancer. The last part of the text suggests the role that music plays in creating *rasa* and describes the rules for instrumental music, vocal singing, lyrical composition, rhythmic permutations, etc. The chapters that pertain to dancing and its experience are selected bearing in mind their relevance to the entirety of *natya*. This study discusses sections of the *Natyasastra* that foregrounds and unfolds the aspect of *rasa*, which is described as the purpose of *natya*.

As a dancer, I question if my experience is the same as the audience experience. Commentaries on *Natyasastra* suggest that *rasa* is the experience of the audience. It invites the question of *what is the dancer's experience called?* The language of *Natyasastra* describes what a dancer is to follow in order to evoke *rasa* in the audience. However, I had unanswered questions on my experience of dancing and if it was also called *rasa*. In order to find language that describes my experience, I explored other traditions of dancing such as modern dance, trance dance, ecstatic dancing, etc. While each style described an experience while dancing, I did not find a language that resonated or worked with my experience of dancing. Dancers such as Anna Halprin described the feeling of oneness with movement but did not have a comparable experience with regards to the interpretive storytelling and emotional expressive aspects central to natya. Trance dancing suggests the movement of the dancer while engaged by a metaphysical entity that manifests as trance. I looked at yoga much later in the search—simply because I had incorrectly considered yoga as a physical practice of postures. However, when I studied the *Yogasutra* I realized that this may be a language that integrated several aspects of my experience in dance.

Yogasutra described the connection between the physical self and a metaphysical other. It outlined eight guiding principles (*ashta anga*) to follow in reaching this communion (*samadhi*). Several scholars have interpreted the principles of *ashta anga yoga* and some have suggested practices that embody these principles. The hermeneutic interpretations of the *ashta anga* principles of yoga provided me with a new language to describe my experience of dancing. My newfound understanding of these eight principles provided an opportunity for a new vision and perspective on the experience of dance. As I processed, analyzed and introspected on this as a heuristic process, further new knowing emerged.

This study makes overt both my process of integrating the information from texts on dance and yoga with my experience of dancing. In this regard, it is important to discuss the hermeneutic interpretations of *Natyasastra* and *Yogasutra* along with their commentaries and supporting literature. It sets the context within which I make meaning of my experience of dance. It provides a different language to describe this experience. It introduces vocabulary that connects the experience of dance with principles of yoga. This facilitates a different understanding of the phenomenological study on the experience of dancing. Hermeneutic interpretation of *Natyasastra* allows the representation that *rasa* is not an unintended or personal aspect of dancing but is the purpose of *natya*. Hermeneutic interpretations of *Yogasutra* introduce the language of *ashta anga yoga* viewed from the perspective of a lifelong dancer.

Dancing in the Middle—Overcoming Limitations

Metaphorically understood, my role as a researcher is to dance between the narrative, heuristic, hermeneutic and arts based aspects of this phenomenological study. My experience of dancing is articulated in the overarching story of my narrative and shared in a different level of depth in the video recordings of several dances. While narrative, arts based and heuristic methods privilege my experience over others, they also allow me to claim authority and validate my experiences as a dancer with over forty years of experience, as a performer with over thirty years of experience and as a teacher with over twenty years of experience.

My initial efforts were to locate documentation of other dancer's experience of dancing, especially *rasa*. I did not find relevant narratives from a dancer's perspective of their inner experience of dancing. This created a need for such a document, even if only for the purpose of this study. My hesitation was on basing my study solely on my experience. How do I know that anyone else feels similarly? How do I establish that this experience can be generalized? If I were to interview a few dancers on their experience of dancing, it would extend my singular opinion to include a few others. It still would not translate into an absolute or irrefutable statement. And, further, this was not the intent of the study.

This study is to share my experiences and suggest at least, one possible explanation for it. The descriptions may create a space of resonance for other dancers, and as such the outcome of the study can be transferrable. Future studies and research may disprove or confirm the validity of my thesis. This study is not intended as the last authoritative statement on the topic of *Natya Yoga.* Instead I chose a hermeneutic approach to discuss that while my experience of dance is unique to me, the *Natyasastra* is clear that the purpose of *natya* is to evoke *rasa*—the experience of dance. I decided to pursue this for two reasons—to demonstrate that *rasa* transcended my individuality and also to explore how the language of *Natyasastra* described *rasa*, especially from the dancer's experience of dancing.

My engagement with the texts of dance and yoga is from my perspective as a dancer. My limited proficiency in Sanskrit prevents direct immersion in the texts. To compensate for this disadvantage, I sought interpretations and commentaries from a diverse field of writers to ensure that I am not limited to any one preferred point of view. In some ways, not having personal and direct knowledge of the texts may work to my advantage. It is conducive to keeping an open mind, while engaging with the interpretations of each writer seeking to find credible grounding and resonance in the composite understandings amongst the various authors. At the same time, I am present to the subjective selection of material I choose to incorporate in this study. The subjectivity of my analysis is an aspect that is made transparent throughout the discussions, especially in the hermeneutic sections. My perspective informs the field of vision I privilege.

As I dance between the heuristic and hermeneutic aspects of my study, I offer readers an exploration of the resonance between the various texts and my experience. My internal compass is tuned to maintaining the integrity of experience that is inclusive of all its complexities. Complexities that are explored through an arts based research and a phenomenological approach. The art based depiction enables the non-verbal expression of multiple aspects that interact in facilitating this complex experience for the viewer and dancer. The phenomenology of dancing experience emphasizes the interrelated dynamics between form and experience in *Bharatha Natyam*.

My dancing embodies the stylized form of *Bharatha Natyam* even while facilitating an experience that is almost mystical and at its core essence, may transcend any one form. This connection between form and its experience is also mirrored in the *ashta anga yoga* where the initial form described in the first four principles (*yama, niyama, asana, pranayama*) connects to the experience of yoga that is described in the next four principles (*pratyahara, dharana, dhyana, samadhi*).

This coexisting dancing form and formless experience is also symbolic of the Apollonian and Dionysian aspects of art. Apollo, the Greek God of beauty is associated with form and structure. Dionysius is associated with mystical experiences and ecstasy that breaks down barriers to "identify the self with the whole of life" (Willcox, 1914, p. 749). Approaching this differently, the study links the form of *Bharatha Natyam* to the practice of *ashta anga yoga;* and the experience of dancing with the experience of meditative immersion in yoga.

Significance of the Study to Yoga

The *Yogasutra* was compiled several hundred years ago and provided guidelines to living by *ashta anga yoga*. Over the years, some yoga practices have emerged that practice aspects of the *ashta anga* principles, such as the breathing, postural and/or meditative aspect. The experience of meditative engrossment (*samadhi*) is sometimes not emphasized as the essence of *ashta anga yoga* practice. My research suggests a renewed understanding of *ashta anga yoga,* based on the original text of *Yogasutra*. This understanding can be applied to several life practices, including *natya*, transforming them into a complete practice of yoga.

Postural practices of yoga have limitations for those who have physical challenges and limited dexterity. Yoga that calls for quiet and calm mindset prior to practice may be difficult for those whose nature is prone to anxiety or higher energy states. My study creates the possibility for yoga practices that are more inclusive of individuals with varying abilities to calm their physical body and mind, while paving a way for them to experience meditative immersion.

Significance of the Study to *Bharatha Natyam*

Bharatha Natyam is presently practiced as creative movement, as an educative and interpretive dance form, and as an entertaining performance. As a dancer, I appreciate the strides that have been made in bridging divides between classical dance styles, both in India and abroad. I am proud of its presence on the international stage—as a dance form that transcends religious, cultural and language constraints. I am excited at the collaborative potential amongst dancers of the world, who are united by the shared experience of dance and movement. In the midst of integration, I am also concerned that the experiential essence of Indian dance may become underrepresented and possibly lost to the dancing world.

Bharatha Natyam when understood as *Natya Yoga* is a therapeutic, spiritual and transcending experience. The richness of its practice has developed over centuries. In the desire to integrate with other world dances, it is important that *Bharatha Natyam* not lose what it has held in its practice for so long. I consider the experience of *rasa* a global treasure that has been well preserved in *Bharatha Natyam*. It is important to me that this dance is not limited to an entertainment or storytelling form. My desire is that my study will reclaim and represent to *Bharatha Natyam* its ability to connect with energies that transcend the dancing self.

Spiritual Significance

Yoga is increasingly recognized as a spiritual practice to stay connected with a larger cosmic presence. Yoga is also understood as a spiritual practice with incidental outcomes such as physical flexibility and medical wellbeing.

In contrast, dance is popularly placed in the category of arts, which can at times represent the sacred. However, several hundreds of years ago, Indian dances were a religious practice (Vatsyayan, 1968). They were performed during religious rituals, as worship to the deity in the temples. Historically, because of foreign invasions, the dances of India turned into entertainment for the monarchs and the larger community. Dances became less religious, and more social in deference to the non-Hindu rulers of India. The religio-spiritual aspect became hidden and over time less represented in Indian dances.

My desire is that my study will reclaim this heritage and represent dance as a spiritual practice whereby we are reminded of our connection to a larger presence. As a performing dance, it also has an ability to include audience in the spiritual experience. While other world dances may have similar qualities, my desire is that this work brings to light the spiritual potential of *Bharatha Natyam.*

Social Relevance

Centuries ago, women dancers were dedicated to temples and danced ceremonially during worship of the deity (Gaston, 1982). Over time, temple dancers became courtesans at the king's palace dancing for entertainment. They were called *devadasi* and socially considered prostitutes (Apffel-Marglin, 1985). It is in recent times, over the past century that their dance in Southern India has been rechristened *Bharatha Natyam* and increasingly practiced by women from other social orders. My study speaks to the discrimination that was placed against women dancers that may still be present in their perceived image as entertainers. My research suggests that dancers have held space for history and spirituality in their dance. It also suggests that dance should be looked upon as treasure house of collective human wisdom, accumulated over centuries and historically documented through the medium of dance. As an appreciative student of dance, I hope my work removes any societal tarnish that may have become deposited, and reclaim what I believe is its essence.

Personal Significance

I searched for language to understand my experience of dance— what was this experience called? How did it come about? Who has talked about it? And, where? As I acquired language to explain aspects of dance, the most obvious missing link that I note is one between the form of yoga and the practice of dance. To bridge this gap and connect the two disciplines is of personal importance. It validates my experience of yoga; it adds credibility to my claim that dance is more than an interpretive art form; it brings together several aspects of my personality—as a healer, a psychotherapist, a dancer, a Yogi, and a teacher/student.

2. LITERATURE REVIEW: BHARATHA NATYAM

The primary focus in this chapter is to establish a strong foundation to support the thesis that the form of *Bharatha Natyam* is an embodiment of *ashta anga yoga* leading to a meditative experience. *Bharatha Natyam* is presently practiced as an interpretive storytelling dance form and its practice has been influenced by several factors such as the history of foreign rule in India. The text of *Natyasastra* documented several centuries ago, *natya*, a predecessor of present day classical Indian dance forms (including *Bharatha Natyam*) was commonly practiced in society.

The *Natyasastra* described various concepts related to the form of *natya* and various emotional expressions in *natya*. However, it did not provide an adequate language to conceptualize the process that facilitates such an emotional experience. This study suggests that the language of *ashta anga yoga* provides additional vocabulary to describe the dancing process.

In this chapter, dance literature is reviewed to study the evolution of *natya* leading to its present form of *Bharatha Natyam*, with emphasis on what has been said about the experience of dancing, called *rasa*. Later chapters continue to discuss in further depth the significance of *rasa* in *natya*, that builds on my narrative and arts based descriptions of *rasa* in *Bharatha Natyam*. Since this study proposes that *Bharatha Natyam*, an integrated dance form is an embodiment of *ashta anga yoga*, Chapter 3 is dedicated to literature review that focuses on other integrated practices of body and mind that are recognized as yoga practices.

Form of Bharatha Natyam

Bharatha Natyam is a classical dance style from Southern India that is practiced as an interpretive storytelling form. Some attribute the word *Bharatha* (also written as *bharata*) to the author of the Indian dance text, *Natyasastra* (Rangacharya, 1986, p. vii). The word *bharatha* is also an anagram of **bha**va (emotional expression), **ra**ga (melody) and **ta**la (rhythm) (Dhananjayan, 1984, p. 8). The Sanskrit word *bharatha* also means actors, suggesting it was a text for *bharatha* (Rangacharya, 1986, p. vii). However, the name of *Bharatha Natyam* as a description of a dance form emerged less than hundred years ago (Kothari, 1982, p. 27).

The form of dancing movements in *Bharatha Natyam* is referred to as *nritta*. Percussive feet reflect the dancer's synchrony with the rhythmic component of the music. This rhythm is pervasive in the dancer's body—the quick arm movements, rapid hand gestures, synchronized with eye movements that punctuate the fluid grace of the entire body. Similarly the melodic aspect of music is emphasized in the graceful body movements that accompany the percussive feet. Some dances are pure movement sequences with no interpretive or expressive purpose, and are referred to as *nritta*.

When *Bharatha Natyam* is used as an interpretive and expressive dance form, the dancer narrates the story from the perspective of a character in that story. The dancer is at times a narrator describing an external story or historical event; at times the dancer becomes the character in the story and expresses the emotional language described in the music. When synchronized with rhythm in music, a dancer is able to experience the emotions in it (*bhava*) (Vatsyayan, 1968, p. 30).

While immersed in that emotional experience, the dancer steps into the role of a storyteller to convey the essence of the experience to an audience—this is the goal of *natya* (Rangacharya, 1986). *Bharatha Natyam* utilizes *hasta mudra* (hand gestures) and *abhinaya* (expression) to convey this emotional experience (*rasa*) to the audience (Vatsyayan, 1968, p. 9). This flow of emotions from dancer's experience through the dancer's expression to evoke audience experience is the premise of *Bharatha Natyam*. The experience of such dancing is called *rasa*.

Natyasastra, written by sage Bharatha is the first text that described dancing movements and expressions as *natya* whose express purpose is to evoke rasa (Vatsyayan, 1968, p. 9). Rasa is described as "neither an object, nor an emotion, nor a concept—it is an immediate experience which relishes its own essence" of the interactions and "communion" while dancing (Daumal, 1982, p. 41). Rasa is described as a mood, sentiment, or flavor that arises when "the taster tastes the taste with taste" (Siegel, 1978, p. 47). The dancer's experience of dancing (*bhava*) is a manifestation of *rasa* (Daumal, 1982, p. 41).

Natyasastra described specific hand gestures used for expressive dance (*nritya / natya)* and rhythmic dance *(nritta)*, feet positions, body movements, emotional experiences (*bhava),* facial expressions (*abhinaya*) to be used to evoke *rasa* (Vatsyayan, 1968). With regard to body movements, *Natyasastra* described specific dance movements, called *karana* that literally means "combination of hands and feet in dance" (Subrahmanyam, n.d.). Dancers sometimes practice *karana* as "frozen movement" misunderstanding them to be "postures and poses" (Subrahmanyam, n.d.). The *karana* descriptions capture a moment in the cadence of dancing movements in *natya* (Rangacharya, 1986, pp. 18–22). There are 108 specific postures described – for example, standing firmly with one foot raised above the head (*harinapluta*), laying face down with body curled into a circular form while on stomach (*sakatasya*), etc. (Rangacharya, 1986, pp. 19–22). Present day form of *Bharatha Natyam* uses movements called *adavu* (considered to a practice of *karana);* patterned combinations of *adavu* danced to rhythm and/or melody are called *nritta. Bharatha Natyam* retains the integrity of some concepts described in the *Natyasastra* such as the hand gestures (*mudra*), feet positions, movements, arm positions, glances of the eye, the emotional characterizations, etc. While some of the practices have changed over time they still correspond with the descriptions in the *Natyasastra*.

The *Natyasastra* is credited to sage Bharatha who must have witnessed numerous dramatic presentations and distilled their essence prior to codifying them as *natya*. At the time *Natyasastra* was written, it is speculated that *natya* was practiced as a dramatized play. However, the form of dance (*nata*) was first referenced in the works of Panini, an Indian grammarian dated around the second century BCE (Rangacharya, 1986, p. vii). Following this early reference to dance, there are no available texts that describe or discuss dancing further, prior to *Natyasastra*. The original treatise of *Natyasastra* is no longer available, and the most recent text used for translations is dated around the seventh or eighth century CE (Rangacharya, 1986, p. vii).

Tracing the evolution of Indian dance over centuries indicates that changing historical factors influenced natya in communities across the country. Historically, foreign rulers who practiced other religions such as Islam, frequently invaded Northern India. *Natya,* which had hitherto reflected prevalent Hindu religious stories and practices adapted in order to continue as an active practice. This form of *natya* that had less emphasis on the storytelling aspects of dance is considered to be an ancestor of present day form of Kathak. Kathak is a classical dance form that emerged in Northern India, between 1300 and 1800 CE and focused primarily on rhythmic movements, devoid of any reference to Hindu gods (Vatsyayan, 1974, p. 84).

Similarly, in other parts of India, existing dance forms adapted to suit the preference of rulers (Vatsyayan, 1974, p. 7). For instance, Odissi was a classical dance form that emerged from the temples of Central India where dancers had retreated to escape persecution by invaders (Vatsyayan, 1974, p. 49). This dance style is distinct for its graceful form, its fluid upper body movements, and its stylized accessories representative of the ethnic jewelry unique to the state of Orissa, where Odissi originates from.

Similarly, in Southern India, there were several dance styles that emerged—*Kuchipudi* in the state of Andhra Pradesh, *Bharatha Natyam* in the state of Tamil Nadu, and *Mohini Attam* in Kerala. The geography of India protected the Southern states from frequent foreign invaders and allowed for *natya* to flourish and adapt to the region it was practiced in. For example, *Mohini Attam* is a graceful and fluid dance style, with the dancers accessorized in garments (*sari*) that were usually in white with gold colored borders. This is reflective of the *sari* commonly worn by women in Kerala.

In contrast, *Bharatha Natyam* is a percussive and dynamic dance style that is an interpretive storytelling form. Focusing attention on *Bharatha Natyam*, there is reference to an art of dancing, called *kuthu* in Tamil language texts such as *Silappadikaram* and *Manimekhalai* dated between 500 BCE and 500 CE (Kothari, 1982, p. 23). Kothari suggested that a classical form of *kuthu* developed into present day *Bharatha Natyam* (1982, p. 23). *Kuthu* in the language Tamil means "dance" and could have been synonymous with the Sanskrit word, *natya*. Tamil was the dominant and spoken language in that part of Southern India that is now Tamil Nadu.

The *Natyasastra* described with great detail positions in dancing that it called *karana*. Sculptural carvings of dancers in such *karana* positions are on the walls of the Brihadishwara temple in Tanjore, a city in Southern India (now Tamil Nadu) that was constructed around the eleventh century CE (Kothari, 1982, p. 23). Piecing together such iconographic images and references in other literature, dancing in Southern India was described mostly in the royal courts where the songs were in praise of the ruling monarch. They were financially supported by the courts and received land, money, cattle, houses, etc. as an appreciation for their art and services. Reviewing the societal role of dancers revealed that dancers in India were employed by Hindu temples and practiced their art as a religious ritual during worship (Apffel-Marglin, 1985). It is possible that while they were also court appointed dancers, their ties were primarily with the principal temple of that region where they practiced their art as worship.

These temple dancers were called *Nithyasumangali* and married to the God enshrined in that temple, and were not permitted to marry another, have children or engage in household life (Gaston, 1982, pp. 6–12). They had a distinct social standing as a *devadasi* (one who serves God). These dancers gained status and became influential in the courts administration. However, they also became socially considered as courtesans and prostitutes, who acted as companions to the king or noble men of the court (Kothari, 1982, p. 13).

In Southern India, the term *devadasi* became almost synonymous with prostitute and their dance was called *Sadir* and *Dasiyattam* during seventeenth to nineteenth century CE (Vatsyayan, 1974, p. 23). In early 1900s, Indian legislature passed the Devadasi Bill that discontinued their employment by temples (Kothari, 1982, p. 27). The art of dance that had been preserved by the devadasi culture became dormant until about 1930 when it was reclaimed and given the status of art, removed from social tarnish of prostitution (Kothari, 1982, p. 28). In 1935, Rukmini Devi entered the dance scene and pioneered the transition into an aesthetic new form, that was renamed *Bharatha Natyam*, and was practiced as an artistic dance form (Kothari, 1982, p. 28).

Present day *Bharatha Natyam* is practiced as a dance form with an educational and artistic value, removed from its previous social tarnish. Several children, primarily girls start learning dance around the age of six or seven years. I started dance lessons at the age of five years and have had the blessing of dance in my life since then. My teachers, Shanta and Dhananjayan, were among Rukmini Devi's first few students and lived with her to learn *Bharatha Natyam*. My experience of learning with my teachers is that dance was the medium through which they taught the art of dancing and living. The techniques of dancing while important are best danced when infused with the spirit of immersion in the dancing experience. This was the path my teachers followed and placed me on. This is the path that has brought me to this present study—to understand how this experience of dancing is evoked and to be able to teach it to another with appropriate vocabulary and language, from across disciplines. The emphasis on an artistic and aesthetic experience of dancing is integral to *Bharatha Natyam*.

This study reclaims its essence of emotional experience and relates this to a transdisciplinary language drawn from multiple texts of dance and yoga. Dance was an integrated practice of worship at temples which later evolved into a communal participatory event. At some point in history, its spiritual practice became separated from its social aspect and *Bharatha Natyam* became a performance for social entertainment and at times, educational. My study seeks to reintegrate the spiritual component and re-vision *Bharatha Natyam* as *Natya Yoga*, where the emphasis is on this form of *natya* that facilitates its meditative experience.

Experience of Natya

The word *Natya* includes acting and dancing— 'dramatic dance' is the closest English translation of the word *natya* (Coomaraswamy, 1985, p. 5). *Natyasastra,* a treatise on *natya* was compiled around 500 BCE (Ghosh, 1981, p. 21). However, the text of *Natyasastra* that is commonly used was re-created from later commentaries, primarily the earliest writings by Abhinavagupta. Additionally, later texts such as *Abhinaya Darpana* based on *Natyasastra* that specifically describe only the dance related aspects reiterate the essence of natya (Ghosh, 1981, p. 1). *Natyasastra* (and *Abhinaya Darpana*) state that the purpose of *natya* is to evoke *rasa* (Ghosh, 1981, p. 6). *Natya* "fulfill(s) a higher end than that of mere entertainment . . . (*natya* provides) . . . liberation from the restless activity of the mind and the senses" (Coomaraswamy, 1985, p. 9). Tiruvenkatachari states in the preface of his translation of *Abhinaya Darpana,* that *natya* "is like *Yogasutra*" (Coomaraswamy, 1985, p. 11).

A seminal thinker and dancer, Vatsyayan, considered that art as yoga achieves a state of complete harmony leading to recognition of one's true self (Vatsyayan, 1968, p. 5). She considered this harmonious experience of the transcendental emotion *rasa* (1968, p. 5). She quoted several branches of Indian philosophy such as *Sankhya, Vedanta,* and Kashmir *Saivism* in saying that scholars like Abhinavagupta, Bhattanayaka, and Srisankuka "agreed that the state of being which this art-experience evoked was a state akin to that of spiritual realization" (Vatsyayan, 1968, p. 7). Abhinavagupta wrote a commentary and translation of the *Natyasastra* titled *Abhinavabharati* around the ninth or tenth century CE and described *rasa* as the "twin brother" of the experience of mystical union in *Samadhi* (Vatsyayan, 1968, p. 7). This is reiterated when Visvanatha said in *Sahitya Darpana* that the nature of *rasa* is "pure, indivisible, self-manifested . . . (and) the very twin brother of mystic experience" (Coomaraswamy, 1985, p. 35). While Udbhata (seventh century CE), Lollata (eighth century CE), Sankuka (eighth century CE), Kirtidhara (ninth/tenth century CE) also wrote commentaries on *Natyasastra,* they "were mostly engaged in refuting one another" and it is unclear if they had "any direct experience with theater" (Rangacharya, 1986, p. xii). While the commentators on *Natyasastra* have included scholars who were not dancers, it is interesting to note that its author Bharatha had written that the *Natyasastra* be used as a *"prayoga sastra"*—permitting comments and changes only by a dancer (Vatsyayan, 1974, p. 25). As a dancer, my experience of dance is consistent with its description by commentators of spiritual realization and mystical experience.

Describing the experience of dance, it is said that "dance is a form of yoga . . .(where the) dancer takes audience to a higher level" (Kothari, 1982, p. 15). Art accomplishes the "purpose of yoga" in "overlooking distinction between subject and object of contemplation"—creating unity of consciousness (Coomaraswamy, 1985, p. 21). In dance, the spiritual import is "*atma* (individual soul) seeking union with *Paramatma* (universal soul)" (Kothari, 1982, p. 76); while yoga is bringing human spirit (*Jivatma*) into constant communication with divine spirit (*Paramatma*) (Kumar, 1998, p. 18).

Approaching from the perspective of yoga, Iyengar, a well known teacher and pioneer in the field of *Hata Yoga* discussed dance as a form of yoga, when he wrote, "Siva is the creator of yoga and dance. . . . The Yogi believes in *nivrtti marga*, the inward path of renunciation; the dancer believes in *pravrtti marga*, the outward path of creation. Yoga is *jnana marga*, a path of knowledge; dance is *bhakti marga*, a path of love" (Iyengar, 1995, p. 144).

Miller (1992) wrote,

In the same way that meditators focus the mind to enter higher states of consciousness, artists in the heat of creating often become so concentrated that self and environment fuse, producing a state of absorption similar to the mystic rapture described in Hindu and Buddhist literature. The focused concentration of both artists and mystics serves to dissolve the ego. (p. 237)

Review of dance literature suggests paucity of writings on the inner experience of dance—of what it feels to be dancing. While there is concurrence of views that the experience of dance is self-transcending, the accompanying literature does not provide supporting details. While experiences may be difficult to describe in words, it is also important to have a vocabulary and develop such a descriptive and suggestive language. The narrative and arts based description of my experience of dancing suggest such a language (in Chapter 4).

The present study suggests that the *prayoga* (practice) of *Bharatha Natyam* can be spiritual and meditative while practiced in its present form, with an added emphasis on awareness of its experience—thus transformed into Natya Yoga. In exploring other languages that speak to such mystical experiences, the vocabulary in *ashta anga yoga* is explored in the next chapter.

3. LITERATURE REVIEW:ASHTA ANGA YOGA

Yoga is a practice that integrates body, mind and spirit; it is also the process of integration that leads to transcendence of physical self. Yoga is the praxis of self-transcendence and union with metaphysical other. Yoga also refers to this union. The root word for yoga, *yuj* means to connect, to link and act as a yoke (Feuerstein, 2003). *Yogasutra,* written by Patanjali was possibly the earliest text on the process and praxis of yoga (Satchidananda, 1990. P. xii). It described eight limbs or *ashta anga* that lead to intuitive knowing and integration of body and mind; seen and seer; matter and energy; *prakriti* and *purusha* (Iyengar, 2008, p. 130). The *ashta anga* described in *Yogasutra* are *yama, niyama, asana, pranayama, pratyahara, dharana, dhyana* and *samadhi.*

These eight limbs (*ashta anga*) provided a guideline for practice of yoga. However, the *Yogasutra* did not name or describe specific approaches that embodied all eight *ashta anga* principles. Various schools of thought interpreted the *ashta anga* and practiced them in their distinctive form. Some were an integrated approach to living and not necessarily practiced in a defined physical form to integrate mind and body. For instance, *karma yoga* was the practice of self-transcending service to other; *bhakti yoga* was the practice of devotion and love; *jnana yoga* was the path of seeking knowledge to self-realization and transcendence. By contrast, some others such as *hata yoga, mantra yoga, laya* and *kundalini yoga* involved using the practice of physical and mental attributes of the body in seeking union (*samadhi*) of the human self with a larger nonphysical entity referred to as *isvara, purusha,* etc. In this chapter, literature review focuses on the latter schools of yoga that incorporate physical form and practice that work towards *samadhi* and self-transcendence through this union.

While the literature review explored the understanding of *ashta anga* principles by various distinct practices of yoga, this study does not attempt to compare *Bharatha Natyam* to any of the other integrated practices. Instead this exploration is undertaken for the purpose of understanding how various yoga approaches interpreted and practiced *ashta anga yoga* to develop a base for this study's suggestion that *Bharatha Natyam* is an embodiment of these *ashta anga* principles of yoga. Academic scholars and *Yogi* have described their understanding of *ashta anga* principles independent of any specific practice of these principles. Chapter 6 is dedicated to a discussion of several such interpretations for each of the *ashta anga* principles of yoga. The present chapter provides the history and context of yoga practices that embody *ashta anga* principles that are further built upon in the following chapters.

Form of Ashta Anga Yoga

The form of yoga as described by the *ashta anga* has aspects of physical practice leading to an internal experience of meditative immersion. The combination of the external form and the resulting internal experience is the path described as *ashta anga yoga*. Vyasa who wrote the first commentary on *Yogasutra* suggested several postural practices for the third *anga—asana*

(Burley, 2000). Texts that came later such as *Gheranda Samhita, Siva Samhita, Vasishta Samhita, Goraksha Shataka, Hata Yoga Pradipika* build on the existing understanding of *asana* as physical postures (Narayanan, 2009, pp. 4–5). While *asana* was recognized as one aspect of the whole *ashta anga yoga,* the word *yoga* has become popularly associated with physical postures, or practice of *asana* (Singleton, 2010, p. 3).

Looking at a broader definition of the yoga, literature review suggests multiple understandings such as, "yoga is ecstasy *(samadhi) (Yoga Bhashya* 1.1); yoga is the union of the individual psyche with the transcendental Self *(Yoga Yagnavalkya* 1.44)" (Feuerstein, 2003, p. 31). Feuerstein described 40 types of Hindu yoga that include: *Karma Yoga,* where the emphasis was on performing one's perceived duty and actions, with a selfless attitude in service; *Bhakti yoga* as yoga of loving devotion and surrender to the Universal Spirit; *Jnana Yoga* as a path of knowledge that leads to self-realization (2003, pp. 36 –38). Another approach, Integral yoga included the latter but also emphasized responsibility for action based on wisdom gained from yoga (Chaudhuri, 1965, p. 43).

Some yoga approaches embodied a way of living that is a practice of self-transcendence, without strict adherence to any specific physical form or meditative experience. By contrast, approaches such as *hata yoga* embodied a physical form that may be mapped to the *ashta anga* principles. For the purpose of this study, since the focus is on understanding how *Bharatha Natyam* embodies the *ashta anga* principles of yoga, literature review focuses on yoga that meet the criteria that "prerequisites of all yoga (practices) are the eight limbs" of *ashta anga* Yoga (Avalon, 1974, p. 186).

"According to *Sivasamhita,* there are four types of yoga practices— Raja Yoga, Hata Yoga, Mantra Yoga and Laya (Kundalini) Yoga" (Kumar, 1998, p. 17). *Raja Yoga* emphasizes the need to control thoughts and mental distractions, in gaining self-regulation and the name suggests that it is the "king of yoga"

(Sivananda, 1960, p. 3). *Hata Yoga* focuses on balancing physical energy within the body and describes various physical postures that align internal energy, in order to commune with external energies (Iyengar, 1995, p. 3). Some practices of *Hata Yoga* overlap with practices associated with *Laya Yoga*, where the physical exercises (postures, breathing, etc.) are used in order to rouse *kundalini* energy within the body, prior to seeking union with the universal energy (Goswami, 1999, pp. 84–85). *Mantra Yoga* uses sound in the form of syllables and phrases to "liberate and control" the thinking mind (Radha, 1980, p. 3). A review of such selected schools of yoga yields several perspectives on each school's understanding and practice of *ashta anga yoga*. It also provides an understanding of how each school builds on different principles of *ashta anga yoga* and helps provide vocabulary for this study's interpretation of *Bharatha Natyam* as an integrated practice of *ashta anga yoga*.

Vocabulary of Ashta Anga Principles

This section provides a working understanding of the eight principles as a frame of reference in understanding how various schools of yoga understand and practice the *ashta anga*. Each principle or *anga* is discussed in further detail in Chapter 6. The discussions here are from the perspective of understanding and developing a vocabulary gathered from the selected schools of yoga. The (eight limbed) *ashta anga* principles described below are a synthetic understanding compiled from proponents of various schools of yoga practice that are discussed in further detail in this and later chapters.

1. *Yama*—ethical values that develop the ability to discriminate and think independently (truthfulness, nonviolence, not stealing, intellectual curiosity, and not being covetous) (Iyengar, 2008).
2. *Niyama*—observances and discipline that facilitate complete practice of yoga (cleanliness, contentment, ridding self of internal impurities, self-awareness, and surrender to the Ultimate) (Mishra, 1973).

42

3. *Asana*—physical practice of postures where body is held steady and balanced, with ease (Rama, 1983, p. 130).
4. *Pranayama*—energizing the body's vital energy by regulation of breath (Satchidananda, 1990).
5. *Pratyahara*—withdrawal of awareness from external sensory stimulation to an inner experience that allows control over sense organs (Sivananda, 1960).
6. *Dharana*—Focused and single-pointed concentration of the mind (Mukherji, 1981, p. 249).
7. *Dhyana*—meditative absorption with a deep sense of oneness between "experiencer and experienced" (Sivananda, 1970, p. 303).
8. *Samadhi*—total meditative immersion where the separation between experiencer and experienced "dissolves" (Kripalvananda, 1977).

While the *Yogasutra* described the *ashta anga* principles, it did not prescribe or define any single practice or integrated approach as an embodiment of the eight principles. *Raja yoga* is considered by many of its practitioners to be the "royal" approach to *ashta anga* yoga and is considered synonymous with it (Rama, 1983). For the purpose of this study *Raja yoga* is considered as an approach that practices *ashta anga* principles towards *samadhi*.

Raja Yoga and Ashta Anga Principles

Raja Yoga is an approach that practices principles of *ashta anga yoga* with the explicit goal of attaining *Samadhi* through control of thoughts and mental distractions (Kumar, 1998, p. 211). Vivekananda wrote that all the *ashta anga of yama, niyama, asana, pranayama, pratyahara, dharana, dhyana* and *samadhi* form the practices of *Raja Yoga* (1998, p. 96).

Swami Sivananda suggested that the practices of *yama,* the first principle of *ashta anga yoga* facilitate control of mental distractions (1960, p. 35).The *yama* (abstinence) values of nonviolence, truthfulness, not stealing, lack of avarice are similarly interpreted by Iyengar (2008, p. 27) and Satchidananda (1990, p.

125). However, there is a difference in the interpretations of the concept of *Brahmacharya* in *Yama* which is commonly interpreted as control of sexual urges in the practice of celibacy, *sanyasa* (Iyengar, 2008, p. 143). It is argued that only when b*rahmacharya* as celibacy is practiced, internal vigor is contained (Satchidananda, 1990, p. 137). However, "repression of sexual energy is not *brahmacharya*, it is freedom from urge" (Sivananda, 1960, p. 35). Swami Rama clarifies that "walk(ing) in Brahman" is *brahmacharya* and it is "not repression and suppression of sexual energy" but having control over its "excess" (1983, p. 123).

The essence of *Niyama* is practiced in the *Raja Yoga* approach by maintaining sanctity and cleanliness of body and mind, and a disciplined lifestyle (Iyengar, 2008, p. 27). When self-motivated to study scriptures with a religious fervor and practiced as an offering to God, the *niyama* concept of *Isvara Pranidhana* is reflected in the individual's lack of attachment to action and its outcome (Satchidananda, 1990, p. 149). This surrender to God paves the way to "perfection" in *samadhi*, the goal of yoga (Iyengar, 2008, p. 148).

Asana is practiced in the *Raja Yoga* approach as steady, comfortable postures or movements (Satchidananda, 1990, p. 152). Iyengar clarified that in his interpretation comfort does not equate pleasure (2008, p. 149). He indicated that reflecting on a physical posture is the true effect of asana that ends "duality between body and mind, mind and soul" (Iyengar, 2008, p. 151). Swami Rama suggested two kinds of *asana* practice—one that is practice of physical postures that leads to the second stage of being able to meditate in a seated position, with neck and spine aligned (1983, p. 130). It interesting to note that while Iyengar's understanding of *ashta anga yoga* principles is consistent with *Raja Yoga's* approach, he is popularly associated with *Hata Yoga*, specifically Iyengar Yoga. It is suggested that *hata yoga* may embody the external physical aspects described in *ashta anga* while paving the way for the internal meditation that is emphasized in *Raja Yoga*.

Pranayama in *Raja Yoga* is practiced as discrete control of inhalation, exhalation and retention of breath and serves to "connect body and mind" (Sivananda, 1960, p. 19). Swami Rama clarified that enhancing the vital energy *(prana)* in the body through breath regulation is *pranayama* (1983, p. 134). When a Yogi was engrossed in mental concentration, a higher level of automatic and responsive breath regulation spontaneously emerged (Satchidananda, 1990, p. 161).

At this state of intense mental control, senses become inwardly drawn by mind (Sivananda, 1960, p. 56) and their stimulation and response are controlled. When senses did not pursue "pleasures from the phenomenal world, they can be yoked to serve the soul" (Iyengar, 2008, p. 159). This aspect of *Pratyahara* or control of senses led to "absolute one-pointedness of mind" or *dharana* (Sivananda, 1960, p. 57). *Dharana* or single pointed focus led to a deeper meditative state in *dhyana* (Satchidananda, 1990, pp. 171–173). *Samadhi* is the highest state of concentration wherein the boundary between self and Universal energy, Isvara is dissolved (Sivananda, 1960, p. 76).

Raja Yoga approach integrates in its practices, the eight principles of *ashta anga* to reach a higher level of meditative immersion. The physical components act as a path to reach the internal mental concentration that facilitates meditation. This seems to be consistent with the premise of *ashta anga yoga*, where the goal is to reach *samadhi* through a meditative absorption that is described in *dhyana*. The path of *Raja Yoga* is using the "intellect to achieve goal of identification with higher reality" (Kumar, 1998, p. 211).

Hata Yoga and Ashta Anga Principles

Hata Yoga is the science of purification (Muktibodhananda, 2000, p. 6). The practices of *hata yoga* balance the energy flow in these two *nadi* and link their flow to a central *nadi* called, *sushumna* (Muktibodhananda, 2000, p. 150). The *sushumna nadi* connects the energies within the body with the pervasive energies on the outside (Finger & Repka, 2005).

Hata yoga (also written *hatha* yoga) developed physical postures as a practice of *asana* to link these energies (Ramacharaka, 1930, p. 9). The *Yogasutra* does not contradict interpretation of *asana* as *hata yoga* postures (Burley, 2000, p. 62), especially since it does not describe any specific set of practices for the *ashta anga* principles. The first mention of postures as practice of *asana* is in the commentary of *Yogasutra* by sage Vyasa wherein he described about a dozen postures that are practiced in a seated position (Burley, 2000, p. 62). Between the sixth and fifteenth centuries CE, other texts such as *Hata Yoga Pradipika, Gheranda Samhita,* and *Goraksha Shataka* added various postures that facilitated energy movement within the body (Muktibodhananda, 2000, p. 1).

In the 1900s, Iyengar developed a branch of postural yoga, Iyengar Yoga, based on *ashta anga* principles of *asana, pranayama* and *dharana* (Iyengar, 1995). Iyengar considered that the importance of *asana* was not just the ability to hold a pose, but to reflect upon it while holding it—he termed this 'repose in pose' (Iyengar, 1995, p. 55). He believed that *Hata Yoga* paved the way to higher practices in the *Raja Yoga* approach, where he described *Samadhi* as a conscious awareness while experiencing transcendence of self-consciousness (Iyengar, 1995, p. 130).

Swatmarama around fourteenth century CE (Burley, 2000, p. 6) compiled the text of *Hata Yoga Pradipika.* This text while building on the *asana* aspect of *ashta anga yoga* also included exercises that focus on retention of *prana,* or life force within the body (Muktibodhananda, 2000). Because of this focus on retention of body vitality, this branch of *Hata Yoga* practice is also considered *Tantric Yoga* (Burley, 2000, p. 16). The practice of retaining *prana* within the body is threefold—by closing orifices through which prana may escape, sealing them by muscular contractions (*mudra*) and locking it within (*banda*) (Burley, 2000, pp. 2–3). The goal of this branch of *hata yoga* was to bring about the union of internal energy (*kundalini*) with the external universal energy (Kumar, 1998, p. 18).

The concept of cleanliness in *niyama (saucha)* informed the *shat karma* cleansing practice in this school of *Hata Yoga* (Muktibodhananda, 2000, p. 2). The *Hata Yoga Pradipika* described practices to cleanse various systems in the body such as digestive tract, circulatory system, etc. (Muktibodhananda, 2000, p. 186). The practice of using breath, postures and natural supplements in cleansing the body is a significant portion of *hata yoga* practices in this school of yoga (Burley, 2000, p. 186).

Asana is described as practice of postures that retained vitality, with the goal of rousing *kundalini* and carrying the energy to the crown of the head, to facilitate union with Universal energy (Goswami, 1999, p. 79). This branch of *tantric / hata yoga* included restraining flow of body fluids, such as semen and considers use of *mudra* such as *vajroli, khecari, etc.* to retain life force (Muktibodhananda, 2000, p. 279).

Hata yoga embodies several aspects of *ashta anga yoga* with focus on the external physical practices that facilitate the union of internal energy with the pervasive external energies. The understanding of *samadhi* appears to be an experience of this communion of energies. While meditative immersion and absorption is suggested in this experience of oneness, the aspect of meditation (*dhyana*) is less prominent than in *Raja Yoga*.

Laya (Kundalini) Yoga and Ashta Anga Principles

Laya Yoga is yoga through rousing *kundalini*—life energy that lies dormant within the body (Kumar, 1998, p. 17). When *kundalini* is awakened, it takes a serpentine path upward through the body to seek union with the universal energy and return to starting position (Goswami, 1999, pp. 84–85). Practices of *mantra, asana*, and *pranayama* in *laya yoga* aim to facilitate a "cosmic intercourse" between internal energy, symbolized by *kundalini* and external energy before returning back to its position at base of spine (Kumar, 1998, p. 210). While conceptually similar to the communion of internal and external energies in *samadhi*, *kundalini* practice involved focus on containing the sexual energy and channeling it through the body via the *sushumna nadi* (Kumar, 1998, pp. 110–112).

In *laya yoga*, interpretation of *asana* was that it may be static or dynamic (Goswami, 1999, p. 47). Dance movements, along with spontaneous *asana* are practiced in *Laya yoga*, which is also called *Kundalini Yoga* or *Shat chakra Yoga* (Goswami, 1999, p. 74). *Shat Chakra Nirupana* is a text that described movement of *kundalini* through *nadi* piercing its way through energy centers (*chakra*) using chants *(mantra)* and associated image *(yantra)* (Avalon, 1974, p. 83).

Kundalini refers to the "potential form of *prana* or life force" (Devanand, 2008, p. 208). Kripalvananda considered *kundalini* the mainstay of yoga and its very entrance (Ishvara, 2002, p. 49). There are two aspects described to activating *kundalini*—the first aspect of which is *pranotthana*, which Sovatsky described as "intensified life energy" (quoted in Devanand, 2008, p. 209). At a higher state of intensification of this energy, there is awakening of *kundalini* in the body, the second aspect of activation. Once the *kundalini* is awakened, it travels up the spine piercing through the *chakra* flowing in the central (spinal) *sushumna nadi* (Ishvara, 2002, pp. 57–60).

Prana is the life energy/breath energy in the body and when the flow of *prana* increases, it refers to *pranotthana* (Ishvara, 2002, p. 54). This strengthening of *prana* can be through a multitude of practices such as serious spiritual practice, or practicing any form of *pranayama* (Ishvara, 2002, pp. 54–57). *Pranotthana* can be an outcome of deliberate and self-disciplined practice; and, can also be imparted by a *guru* (teacher) to a student (Tirth, 1997, p. 1). The latter is a practice of *Shaktipat* that is a means of awakening the *kundalini* by "transmission of spiritual energy" by the *guru* (Tirth, p. 2). *Shaktipat* is also described as "the process by which a master leads prepared students to higher levels of consciousness" (Tigunait, 1996, p. 168).

Sovatsky considered *pranotthana* as a "heightened condition" of the *prana* that manifests as a glow in the face of children, pregnant mothers, musicians while performing with excitement, etc. (Sovatsky, 2009, p. 256). Once the *kundalini* is activated, it manifested as spontaneous sound (*anahata nad*), movements and yoga posturing (*sahaja yoga*) (Sovatsky, 2009, p. 256). The suggestion was that the body movements, positions, change in breath and other physical actions may be a manifestation of the awakening and movement of *kundalini* along the body. Jnaneshvar compared these spontaneous actions (*asana, mudra*) to the (innocent) body movements of children (Sovatsky, 2009, p. 256).

Laya Yoga embodies the experience of union that *ashta anga yoga* describes as its goal in *samadhi*. The ability to remove self from the spontaneous movement of *kundalini* is representative of the key element of *Isvara pranidhana* which removes the sense of "I-ness" and creates an enhanced "sense of perception" and experience (Tirth, 1997, pp. 3–4).The integrated *laya yoga* practice of *asana* as postures and movement, *pranayama* as energizing the vital force of *prana* within the body, along with *mantra*—are in service of the central goal of awakening *kundalini shakti* that lies within the body. Once awakened, *kundalini* spontaneously moves towards an union with the external energies, before returning to the base of the spine. This is the experience of *samadhi* in the practice of *kundalini yoga* that is also the goal of *ashta anga yoga*.

Mantra Yoga and Ashta Anga Principles

Mantra is a syllable, sound word or set of words intuited by great *Yogi* and not a language in which human beings speak (Ajaya, 1980, p. 84). The word *mantra* means "the thought that liberates" from a phenomenal world (Radha, 1980, p. 4). Mantra is a thought sound (such as *hreem, shreem, Om,* etc.) that is used to quiet mental activity and thinking and shift awareness inwards (Bloomfield, 1975, p. 17). *Mantras* have energy in them called *bija* (Radha, 1980, p. 5) and all *mantras* have "equal potency or power"

(Sivananda, 1952, p. 1). The natural sound of human breath is 'so hum' while the "seed mantra of universal consciousness" is "Om" (Tigunait, 1996). The goal of *mantra yoga* is to achieve "unity of individual consciousness with cosmic consciousness" (Radha, 1980, p. 6). When *mantras* are repeated, this recitation (silent or aloud) is called *Japa* (Sivananda, 1952, p. 1). *Japa* practice "steadies the mind . . . (and) . . . unites devotee with Lord . . . (it) awakens *kundalini*" (Sivananda, 1952, p. 1).

Maharishi Mahesh Yogi developed use of *mantra* in his methodology of Transcendental Meditation (TM). Each person has an individual thought sound (*bija mantra*) that works to counter their personal mental process, and thereby stills their mind (Bloomfield, Cain & Jaffe, 1975, p. 17). TM is a meditative process of observing thoughts that "bubble to the surface" and the use of *bija mantra* calms down mental activity (Bloomfield, Cain & Jaffe, 1975, p. 13).

Similarly, Finger and Repka suggest utilizing of specific syllables, called *bija mantra*, which are monosyllabic sounds and correlates each to specific energy centers in the body called *chakra* (2005). Specific *bija mantra* access energy at that *chakra* (Avalon, 1974, p. 83). Mantra can be repeated aloud (*vaikari mantra japa*), in whispers (*upamsu mantra japa*), silently *(manasika mantra japa)* or in written form (*likuta mantra japa*) (Radha, 1980, p. 8). Mantra repetition (*japa*) can be done even while engaged in other activities, including postural practice of *asana* (Sivananda, 1952, p. 73; Radha, 1980, p. 111). Sivananda clarified that "mental *japa* of *Om*" is more powerful than "verbal *japa*" (1960, p. 28).

Mantra yoga embodies *ashta anga yoga* in its dedicated focus (*dharana*) on shifting awareness inwards (*pratyahara*), thereby facilitating a quiet mind that is conducive to meditative engagement. It emphasizes the power of *mantra japa* to focus internal energies and quiets the mind, so that the practitioner's awareness is entirely on the inner experience that is consistent with the goal of meditative immersion (*dhyana*) described in *ashta anga yoga*.

When the concept of *mantra* is expanded to include rhythm and melody, it leads to the practice of music. When music is practiced as a form of yoga, it is referred to as *Nada* Yoga. A musician who is a practitioner of *Nada Yoga*, is described as one who has the ability to "hear" inaudible sound (*nada*) and manifest it as music (Dey, 1990). *Nada* is described as the potential or cause for audible and inaudible vibrations—it is described as causal sound that creates images and spoken syllables, such as *mantra* (Dey, 1990, p. 6). There are four distinct stages described in the translation of potential *nada* into audible *nada*, namely *para* (transcendent potential—inaudible), *pashyanti* (visualized— heard by the mind, for example - in dreams, etc.), *madhyama* (ex. whispers) and *vaikari* (audible) (Avalon, 1974, p. 88). A sophisticated musician is described as one whose musical skills have created an inner pathway for communion with the external energy of *nada* (Ramakrishna, 2005).

From this communion and synergy music emerges—it is this musical energy that a dancer resonates with. Without the synergy and emotional experience of music, the dancer is limited in manifesting the dancing potential of *nada*. In the words of Rukmini Devi, a dancer whose "inspiration comes from music" is very different from another who does not respond or understand the energy of *nada* in music (Kothari, 1982, p. 13). A renowned musician and scholar, Sambamoorti stated that music adds "three values" to dance—musical value, rhythmic potential and the lyrical literary content (Kothari, 1982, p. 19). These elements of *nada* act as "the essential supporting pillars" of *natya* (Dey, 1990, p. 60).

I propose that *Natya Yoga,* similar to *Raja Yoga* embodies the eight principles of *ashta anga yoga*; shares the element of physical practice with *Hata Yoga*; emphasizes the element of *nada*, as does *Mantra Yoga*; and employs a dialogical interaction between *Jeevatma* and *Paramatma*, similar to the concept of *Shakti/Purusha* interactions of *Kundalini Yoga*. This study will explore in depth how *Bharatha Natyam* is a form of yoga, and embodies principles of *ashta anga* yoga leading to meditative oneness.

APARNA RAMASWAMY

4. DANCER ON DANCING: EXPERIENCING BHARATHA NATYAM

Bharatha Natyam is an interpretive storytelling dance form— or, so I had thought, up until this present study on experience of dance. My experiences as a dancer and teacher have led me to question my limited understanding. I began to wonder if the interpretive aspect is but an attribute of *Bharatha Natyam*—one that has been nurtured over time. Per the dictates of *Natyasastra*, *natya* is performed to create an aesthetic experience (*rasa*) in the viewer. The *prayoga* (practice) of *Bharatha Natyam* based on this understanding strives to create *rasa* in the spectator. The dancer's use of expressive movement, gestures and facial expressions is to convey the essence of dance to the spectator, creating *rasa* in an involved observer.

Dancer's Curiosity

As a therapist, I now wonder what else dancing facilitates, especially for the dancer. While dancing for the audience, what is the dancer's experience? How does the dancer experience the engagement with dance? Is the experience different when not performed for spectators? How does the dancer's experience of movement relate to the experience of emotions? What is the role of an involved audience in a dancer's experience of dance? What is the dancer's experience of dancing called?

To set the stage for the journey described in this study, this chapter introduces my role as I enter the arena. This chapter is written in the style of a narrative where I dance between describing events in a chronological sequence and lingering while expressing and tentatively languaging my experience of dance. The written part of this chapter provides an underpinning for an arts based video recording that follows. In this video documentation, a variety of dances are shared for further exploration of experience of dancing in Chapters 7 and 8.

Dancing Despite Myself

Bharatha Natyam found me when I was about five years old. As I recollect, I was mostly indifferent to dance, and more interested in sports and playing games with friends. Dance classes meant time spent away from after school fun. It involved travel time to and from classes, it meant following rules set by the dance teacher, it represented tedium. And classes were three times a week. It meant not watching a movie on television—at the time, we only had a few hours of broadcast a week. It meant getting back on a public bus to get to class and at times on a weekend day while the rest of the family relaxed and took naps. So, why did I persevere? Frankly, the thought of discontinuing never occurred to me. Instead, I thought that learning dance entailed years of tedious work, with little pleasure. I now wonder if that is the reality of learning an art form that focused on repetition to develop artistry and technical perfection.

As students, we spent several years learning and practicing basic movements until our dancing did not involve conscious thinking, or deliberate concentration. It became a part of me. I would dance movements as I walked around at home. I would gesture as part of my conversations. I even mastered the art of daydreaming while dancing intricate and fast paced movements. Dance became my language—it was how I communicated. It created my identity—I was a dancer.

Loving The Lights

After eight years of tedious work, my teachers deemed me ready to step into the world of performing. It presented a dancer shaped by years of dedicated practice—and the vision was glamorous. The vision was one of a *Bharatha Natyam* dancer accessorized in shimmering silk and gold sari, brilliant gold jewelry with sparkling stones, beautiful drawn eyes, colorful lips, fragrant flowers adorning long braided hair—dancing center stage in a brightly lit dancing hall. The attentive gaze of musicians, an involved audience, supportive family and friends were all directed towards the dancer and dance. This was a heady and powerful experience.

There was hard work that was behind this vision. In *Bharatha Natyam*, while the debut performance is often viewed as the culmination of learning, in reality it was the beginning of another kind of learning. It was learning how to perform on a stage. It was learning how to perform this dance form to an audience. It was learning to engage and communicate to a group of individuals, nonverbally.

I learned complex rhythmic sequences that demanded mastery of music comprehension—to understand how rhythm was woven into melody; to synchronize with music; to be attentive to artistry; to be present to the audience; and above all, to understand the responsibility of representing myself, my teachers, and the art of *Bharatha Natyam*.

Rhythm came easy to me—expressions too. The challenge was to experience emotions authentically, so that its expression was genuine. I learned to dance the roles of women who were older than me—women who danced their love and passion for their beloved; women who danced their pain of separation from their beloved; women who surrendered to their beloved. I learned dances about religious beliefs; dances of surrender to God; dances that narrated history, mythology and nature; dances that described love stories; dances that educated and encouraged the spectator to practice conscientious living.

As a teenager, I had minimal frame of reference for these emotions and yet, as a *Bharatha Natyam* dancer I had to strive for authentic experience so that its expression was genuine. As I reflect, I wonder where that emotional energy came from. I wonder what made it possible to feel emotions that didn't come from my life experiences at the time. I had an active imagination, but this called for access to an entirely different emotional knowing. I wondered what made it possible—what allowed dancers like me to access this knowledge and experience?

Shaping My Dancing Self

As a solo dancer, I developed my identity as a communicator—to focus on audience resonance with my dancing. I became aware of dancing with musicians, whose music resonated with me—whose music evoked dancing—who were able to create rich emotional experience in their music. At those moments, it was effortless to synchronize with the music—I could feel the intensity of their musical experience. I was able to experience the emotion, even those I didn't quite understand, cognitively (at the time). My dance was an expression of my experience. As the audience engaged and responded, it amplified my own experience of dance and the music. I found myself enjoying some audiences more than others; appreciating selected venues; and harmonizing better with some musician's rendition of a song. At times of such harmony, the experience of dancing seemed pronounced for the audience, deeper for the dancer (me) and created a richer interaction.

I realized my experience of dancing was always in the moment. I could reflect later, on how I felt during a certain moment of a dance but it became futile to dance trying to recapture that same moment or experience. I realized that it was co-created at a given moment in time by the group of observers and participants, present at that moment. I understood that the experience of dancing is new and unique to each dancing event.

Dynamic Duo

While I enjoyed the individual experience as a solo performer, concurrently I was involved in several group presentations with my dance mates. When we danced as a duo presenting solo dances, the experience in a sense was still individual. We took turns depicting some movements, appreciated the other dancer and worked together to present a harmonious dance. The responsibility to create an aesthetic experience in the audience was shared. At times, the audience feedback—their aesthetic experience was not strong. The focus seemed to shift to aesthetic presentation of a dance, and less on experience of it. As a dancer, while my attention was on my role as communicator, a larger portion of my focus was on stage position, artistry in comparison to the others, ensuring that I depicted my assigned portion of the dance and allowed the other to do the same. Sharing the stage also meant less ability to influence audience experience and somehow this seemed to dilute my own experience of dancing.

Presenting thematic group dance drama entailed intensive rehearsals to ensure coordination. The focus was on demonstrating the choreography in its complexity and intricacy. The dancer carried the responsibility of conveying the personality and emotional state of the portrayed character. As a lead role, I felt able to act the part for a longer duration. I was able to stay as the character and immerse myself in that role. My responsibility was to the convey how the character felt, and responded—to dance all of what I understood and experienced as the portrayed character. In such thematic presentations, I was able to savor the character's personality for longer periods of time. I was in my late teens during this time and I had accessed other resources such as movies, books, etc. While I could place myself in the role of the character, how dancing facilitates stepping into such emotional states was still not explained.

As A Courtesan

Using an experience as example to illustrate this better, I was cast in a lead role for a thematic dance production, wherein I danced the role of a courtesan. The courtesan was a powerful woman in the king's court—the king and other noblemen were enamored of her beauty and she had all that she desired. At least, up until she fell in love with a Buddhist monk. The story goes on to develop how at the end of her life, when her physical appearance was marred, her suitors had abandoned her. It was the monk who gave her emotional and spiritual solace and stayed by her side till her end, although not as her lover.

Stepping into this role, I was able to depict the proud arrogance of a beautiful woman—I had seen similar depictions in Indian movies. I could even depict the pain of rejection by the beloved—I had read several romance novels to fuel my imagination. But when I depicted what she felt at the end of her life, my experience was intense. I experienced her exhaustion, her disillusionment, her emerging understanding of love, her experience of being loved and held by the monk whom she had desired, her acceptance of dying, her calm and peace—emotions I could not attribute to anything I had consciously experienced.

Taught By Students

Where does this experience come from? Was it in me? Or, was it in the music? Where did it reside? Was it created through dancing? By this time, I had grown comfortable with not knowing how this experience was created within me. I had accepted not understanding where my experiences came from. This held true until I stepped into the life role of a teacher.

My youngest students were about the same age I was when I started dance lessons—around five years old. It was important to me that learning seemed less tedious to my young students. I wanted them to question what they were learning and persevere till they had answers that were acceptable to them. I wanted them to understand that interpretive storytelling was the basis of *Bharatha Natyam.* I reiterated the need to strive for authentic experience prior to learning expressive methods. I reinforced that expression without genuine experience was simply making faces.

Of course, as five years olds, they paid no heed to all that I wanted them to know. What engaged them was wearing colorful clothes, sparkling accessories, dancing on stage for friends and family, being photographed and videotaped by enthusiastic parents. I realized learning can happen only when the student is ready for it. I responded to their enthusiasm by creating simple dance sequences using basic movements. In practicing for a performance, they found motivation to repeat movements and correct mistakes. And while correcting their positions and movements, I found the meaning in these dances. I was able to enjoy the beauty of rhythm and the grace of movements—from the outside. I could appreciate what the audience received from dancing. I developed respect for the dancer, dancing and my teachers. I understood why my teachers had taken so much time laying my dancing foundation. I understood that my body's memory and recollection of movements needed to get flow naturally, without deliberate concentration and focus on 'what' I was dancing. It was only then, could my awareness and attention shift to 'how' I was dancing.

When teaching expressive dance, I struggled to provide examples that my young students could relate to. I suggested comparable experiences that they could draw upon. I explained the context, setting, personality and emotional state of the characters in the story. For example, while narrating how a character feels rejected or not included, I would remind them of how it feels when a friend does not include them in a game, or when they are last to be picked for a partner in a project. I would act like a speaker at the podium, reading a script written by another. I asked them how they acted when making their point to a disbeliever or persuading a parent about the merit of their request. I acted how passionate their words would be when they believed in what they were saying. I would draw a parallel to how engaged they need to be in their own dancing, if the expectation was to engage an audience. There were occasions when I would act out a character and ask them to emulate. However, I used imitation mostly as a way to demonstrate a student's innate ability to express feelings facially. I encouraged individual experience and expression.

Spoken Dance

I noticed that language of lyrics limited audience ability to comprehend, especially in the US where both audience and dancers were fluent primarily in English. I found it inappropriate to have a young student dance romantic songs. I felt it was unnecessary to use religious dances to highlight the artistic nature of *Bharatha Natyam*. I choreographed dances on nature, on relationships that were not romantic (with parents, friends, with self) and when possible used English voice over to facilitate understanding of words.

While it was well received and I had significant success from these ventures, I had lost my connection with dance. These dances didn't speak to me. My experience of dancing became superficial and unsatisfying. In my desire to make *Bharatha Natyam* more accessible, I may have lost sight of its essence. I felt I was at a dead end—I stopped dancing.

I became a story-teller of a different kind—with spoken words. I narrated mythological stories with a new perspective, broadcast on public television. I maintained the integrity of the original story while showing its relevance to present day living. I choreographed thematic presentations on stories that I resonated with. For example, I read an old epic, Ramayana and heard in it something different. The story is about Prince Rama's life journey from childhood till he was crowned king several years later. The story narrates the choices he makes as a duty bound son, as a loving husband, a reliable protector of his people, and so on. When I read it with fresh eyes, I saw that the poet wrote the story as narrated to him by Rama's wife, Sita. The story was really a narration of Sita's experience of Rama. It was Sita's story and I choreographed a thematic dance presentation titled Sita's story. It allowed me to highlight that Sita was an empowered woman, single mother, educated, duty bound but assertive and so on. It allowed me to use the medium of *Bharatha Natyam* to convey a message that has special relevance for many of the young girls and women growing up in the United States, at times saddled by traditions and their interpretations.

I had segued into dance as a therapeutic tool for influencing minds. As a psychotherapist, I saw the value of movement in therapy. And yet, I felt *Bharatha Natyam* was more than movement. It was more than an expression of experience. It was more than a carrier of cultural messages. It was more than an art form. There was more to it than the stylized movements. My experience of *Bharatha Natyam* was not explained by a language, at least not any that I knew.

Languaging Experience

I had come full circle - what was this experience that I felt while dancing? Answering this question is similar to answering 'how does food taste?' - it depends on the cuisine, on a specific dish, the recipe used that day, the eye and the hand that cooks, the ambience of the dining area, the mood and appetite of the person engaging in the eating experience. My experience of dancing rhythmic movement is different from expressing emotions. My experience of dancing to live orchestral accompaniment is unlike dancing to prerecorded music. My dancing experience as a performer is qualitatively distinct from how it feels while practicing in private. And each experience is tempered by a varying set of environmental, physical and emotional factors that interact on any given day. My dancing experience is unique and exclusive to a dancing moment, defined by variables in time and space.

When I use the word experience, it includes at least two distinct qualities to me. One is the action—my engagement with the act of dancing—my absorption and immersion in dancing. The second is my awareness of my engagement—my appreciation of the absorption—my experience of the immersion. While immersed, there is only a state of being in that moment. The appreciation of that moment automatically suggests a different kind of absorption—an absorption that accommodates an observing aspect of my self. When I dance, I find that I move freely between these two states of absorption. Even while completely engrossed in the dance, there are moments when I am aware that I am immersed in the emotion. During those moments, there is simultaneous presence of an immersion and appreciation of the immersion. In the sections that follow, while describing my experience I dance between these co-existing states of absorption and awareness.

Flat-Footed Grace

While dancing percussive rhythm, the sole of my feet that were shaped quite flat became a strength - when my foot struck the ground, it managed to make a loud slapping sound. This served to express the rhythmic beat maintained and performed by my feet. It conveyed firmness, precision and strength - it may have even suggested tremendous effort. Yet, it was my natural way of striking my feet - it took more effort for me to restrain the movement or limit the sound. And, the unintended outcome was the steady posture of my legs that allowed me to raise my feet without having to substantially lift my knee or shift my balance. Using my arms involved more effort - in holding a precisely outstretched arm position or in lifting my elbows while holding my hands at chest level. I was able to somehow hold firmly the hand gestures (*mudra*) used for rhythmic dances - it felt like a natural expression of the arm movement. The rhythmic element (*nritta*) of *Bharatha Natyam* could be danced to melodic music or only to the rhythmic beats. When danced to highlight rhythm, percussive drumming, cymbals and musician's vocal prompts supported the dancer. During these depictions, the melodic support was silent. However, when the emphasis was on demonstrating rhythm that is inherent in melody, there were no vocal prompts and the entire orchestra was responsive to both rhythm and melody - in an integrated musical rendition.

When dancing to rhythmic beats my body's response to the vocal prompts was to depict precision of movement. My dance with the percussive rhythm was to demonstrate competence and mastery of speed. My initial experience of rhythmic movement was that it took significant memory to remember the exact order and combination of dance sequences. My involvement was with 'what' I was dancing. With increasing certainty and easy recollection of 'what' to dance, I found my attention slowly shifted to 'how' to dance.

I became engrossed with the steady balance in my posture, moving my arms with precise grace, ensuring synchrony with music, with accentuated awareness of the visual and aesthetic experience of rhythmic dance. My attunement was to the rendition of vocal prompts by the musician (often it was my teacher) and the percussive engagement of the drumming. My enjoyment was in the precise and graceful synchrony between dancer, musician, and rhythm.

Movement in Music

When it came to melodic music my body responded differently to melody. The dance became pronounced in its fluidity and grace. Dancing to melody called for increased concentration to discern and emphasize the inherent rhythm in the lilting melodies. However, response to the songs seemed to stretch out the movement between its rhythmic start and end of the beat. Whereas, in rhythmic music, the precision emphasized the rhythmic starting and ending points of each arm and leg movement.

Using a geometric example, dancing to rhythmic music was more like marking bold dots as if to establish that rhythm was about its position. The dancing movement started precisely on beat (at a dot) and ended precisely on beat (at a dot). While the dancer needed to move her body between these dots, the emphasis was not on how she connected the dots.

In contrast, while dancing to melodic music, the movement between these dots was the emphasis. While the dots still provided form, the focus was on the graceful connections that were made. The flowing movement of the lines, arcs, and curves created the dancing canvas.

My attunement in melodic music was to my internal focus on keeping count and my enjoyment was in the fluidity of dancing movements, a response to the melodic nuances in the singer's voice, and accompanying musical instruments.

Watching the beauty and grace of other dancers, I appreciated the vibrancy of the visual experience of rhythmic dancing. It exhilarated and brought a smile to my face - watching the agility, precision and speed of dancing. It relaxed my body even as I moved in response to the dancer's flowing grace in movements. My eyes tracked their feet; I was mesmerized by the arms and followed eye movements, as if in a trance. Every time I danced, I knew what I was striving to recreate for my audience. I danced so they could feel what I felt, both as a dancer and as an appreciative spectator. I danced to convey the beauty of melody, the precision of rhythm—their intensity amplified by the energy of dancing body movements.

While performing to a live orchestral accompaniment, some of my attention was engaged by the variables in music - ensuring compatibility and synchrony between dance and music. The audience experience of live accompaniment seemed deeper, watching the interactions amongst musicians and with dancer. The music assumed a different quality when the musician felt the appreciative response from the audience. This enhanced the dancer's experience of music, and thereby the dancing experience for all.

While using pre-recorded music allowed for mobility and ease of rehearsals, it did not generate a comparable experience for the audience. For the dancer, since the music was rehearsed, the nuances and emotions were anticipated and the dancer's depictions were in some ways premeditated and deliberate. However, it was possible to set a higher expectation for the quality of prerecorded music as opposed to the performance uncertainties of live orchestral music.

This aspect of musical certainty played an important role especially in expressive dances. The singer's organic experience of the music sets the emotional bar for dancing. While dancing to music where the singer's experience was moderate, it was difficult for me to experience deep or intense emotions. In these circumstances, dancing to a superb recording can facilitate a higher degree of intensity and experience of emotions. Especially when used in smaller dancing halls, where the audience is seated closer to the dancer. However, when dancing in large spaces, the experience with a live orchestra outweighed the advantage of superb prerecorded music.

Dancer on Dancing

To me, dance is my emotional experience of dancing and expression of this experience. When I step into the role I portray, for those few minutes I transform into that person. I understand the personality, outlook, emotions, insecurities, thinking and emotional state of that character. It becomes real to me - I become the character - it is me. I am not acting—I am being that person. I am not pretending - I am experiencing that person. I am not imitating - I am expressing what I genuinely feel at that moment. The work involves understanding the setting, context, character and the circumstances of the story that is narrated. This facilitates stepping into the role—to become that person and experience what is felt, respond accordingly, engage in dialogue true to the character's personality and emotional state.

In dances that are a first person narration, it is rewarding to stay in the role of the character for the entire duration of the dance. From the moment I prepare to dance - I hold my body consistent with the character's frame of mind and personality. As I walk onto the stage, even before anything has been said, there is communication about who 'I' am in the dance. While on one level, I am acting the part - it is more of an enactment of my experience of that role. The emotions are true, my feelings intense, my interactions real and my experience authentic. When enacting a dialogue between a woman and her beloved, if she feels betrayed - I feel her betrayal. I respond by crying her tears, feel her anger, the accusations, sarcasm, and hurt pain until such time that I feel ready to move into a reconciliatory space. While the lyrics provide the structure and framework, the authentic depiction of the character brings alive the interpretive dialogue and story of the dance.

In dances, where there are two or more characters depicted by the dancer, the narration uses second person (and third person) language. While the experience of the narrator provides a way to step out of the character portrayed, it limits the extent to which the dancer can be absorbed in the experience of the character. For example, if I were dancing a story where the narrator approaches her friend's beloved and describes to him how unhappy and distraught her friend feels—while depicting the friend, I would have the opportunity to immerse myself in her longing for him, feel the pain of her separation from him, feel her despair and cry her tears. However, I would have to step back into the role of the narrator and separate from this immersion. In my role as the narrator, I would feel the helpless concern that she feels for her friend, her eagerness to bring relief, her urgency in asking the beloved to reach out to her friend. While dancing such dual roles, it provided me an understanding of how emotional experiences feel on the inside and how others experience them from the outside. In many ways, this was similar to my understanding of how the dancer on the inside experiences movements, and how the audience from the outside appreciates them.

The challenge was in depicting dances in third person descriptive narrative. For example, describing the beauty and grandeur of a temple or the serenity of sunset by the riverside - while the words described the beauty, what gave the depiction life was the energy of the viewer. How was the beautiful scene experienced by the narrator, what was the response felt from the experience - this was what gave relevance to the depiction of beauty. If I saw the scene in my mind's eye and felt present in it, I could express its beauty of the words as I saw it. I could show how cooling the gentle breeze felt to my skin; I could show the beauty of moonlight as it bounced off the river; I could share my enjoyment of the chirping birds singing their evening song; I could depict the entirety of my experience. This called for an ability to place within the scene depicted and experience the breeze, moonlight and singing birds.

My dancing was infused with energy when performing to an audience, even if it were just one person at a rehearsal or practice session. The attentive engagement of the onlooker evoked a response in me, as I danced for them. When dancing for myself, while my understanding and experience of the song remained comparable - my experience of dancing was different. I was not as attentive to *mudra,* postures, movements or interpreting. I was not overly concerned about the intensity of my own experience - it happened spontaneously on occasion. Mostly, it felt like a practice of movements, an exercise in memory with a different kind of engagement.

Being Danced

While listening to songs that resonated with me, I would sometimes stop dancing. I would sit down and continue dancing in my mind. Moving my body seemed to be simply an expression of my inner dancing - in those moments, my experience of dancing as one of complete resonance. I would sometimes close my eyes, the music would make me smile with delight, my body and head would sway of their own accord, the words and melody would touch me to my core. At its most intense, I was not aware of my self - that I was listening to music, or I was seated; I was not aware of the words in the music; I was at times not even aware of the music; I was immersed and taken over by the emotional energy. There were fleeting moments when I was aware of my immersion - it was in these moments that I savored the emotional richness of my experience. I noted my engrossment in the emotion - I delighted in my experience. It was in those moments that I relished my immersion experience.

But there were times when it was just the experience without any attempt to savor it. At these times, since my attention was not on relishing it, I was free to immerse and be enveloped by the emotional energy of the song. I could just be—without feeling an urge to do anything more. While dancing, there were times I experienced my dancing and mostly, it was a sense of being in the moment, without introspection or analysis. It was a state of heightened awareness.

Arts Based Depiction

Please view the video documentation of my dancing titled Bharatha Natya Yoga – an embodiment of *ashta anga yoga*

http://natyayogatherapy.net/bharathanatyayoga/

Burning Questions

My journey has been to understand this state of experience— one of heightened awareness, where I am aware of my physical space even while immersed in an experience that seems to transcend me. An experience that envelops me, even as I dance synchronized with music, interpreting and sharing with the audience.

Natyasastra describes the depiction of various emotional states in *natya* that evoke a corresponding aesthetic experience (*rasa*) in audience. *Rasa* is that which can be savored; it's a flavor that can be tasted; it's an experience that can be relished. However, *Rasa* also suggests an awareness - a self that is able to delight in the emotions experienced; a self that enjoys its immersion.

This invites the question - how can taste manifest without the act of tasting? Can each be experienced without the other? Conceptually, while the two may exist independently, is *rasa* their co-existing experience?

Pertaining to dancing, is a dancer's immersion in dance *rasa*? Or, does it also include the dancer's experience of that immersion? And, can immersion be experienced without an awareness of its presence? What does the *Natyasastra* say about *rasa* and *natya*?

5. NATYA & RASA: UNDERSTANDING THE MESSAGE IN NATYASASTRA

My quest to understand the phenomenology of dancing took me to Indian traditional texts. But this journey has not followed a straightforward trajectory. I bought my first copy of a commentary on *Abhinaya Darpana* when I became a dance teacher twenty years ago. The *Abhinaya Darpana* is a text that distilled from the *Natyasastra* essential dance concepts and terminology that relates to *natya*. I reviewed Ghosh's interpretation of *Abhinaya Darpana* feeling a need to confirm my recollection of what I had learned when I was a student and to review the Sanskrit verses that described hand gestures (*mudra*), and their use in expressive dance. At the time, I was not drawn to do any further review of related texts. The present study however has necessitated a re-engagement with the textual material of Indian dance, specifically texts that speak to the phenomenology of dancing and its experience. This chapter reviews commentaries and interpretations of *Abhinaya Darpana* and *Natyasastra* from a dancer's perspective to reconcile the written descriptions of form of *natya* with the practice and experience of *Bharatha Natyam*.

The earliest mention of dance in Indian literature is in the writings of Panini, a grammarian who lived in India around third century BCE. Panini refers to dance as *nata*, and makes reference to a text called *Nata Sutra* written by Silalin and Krsasva (Rangacharya, 1986, p. vii). Other texts from that time period indicate that Kohala, Tumburu, and Dattila were considered authorities in theater, music and dancing (Pande, 1997, p. 17). However, the first comprehensive text on Indian dance, music and theater was the *Natyasastra* even though it was not necessarily the first on the subject (Rangacharya, 1986, p. ix). Later commentaries, interpretations and translations of *Natyasastra* form the basis of its present day understandings.

The various textual interpretations of *Natyasastra* agree on most of the descriptions of terms discussed therein. For the purpose of this study, I am using Rangacharya's interpretation and commentary as a guide, and where appropriate I present different perspectives from other authors. This is not to suggest that Rangacharya is the authoritative commentator on *Natyasastra*. Instead, I am limiting myself to one text as a main reference, and will include other opinions, understandings and interpretations to supplement it. When I refer to texts in plural, I am making reference to multiples texts (commentaries, translations, and interpretations) that are based on *Natyasastra* and not to any particular text.

Positioning Myself in This Hermeneutic Dance

This study has a particular aim. I am attempting to find where within the Indian tradition one can find the language that best capture the multiple dimensions of dancing—its sophisticated form and subtle experience. I sought words that speak to the phenomenology of dancing. I sought vocabulary that languaged the entirety of *Bharatha Natyam* as a dance form and as a practice. It is with this intent that I engaged and entered the hermeneutic horizon of *Natyasastra* and explored how the written language reconciled with the practice and experiential language of dancing. Since the focus of this study is on the form and experience of *Bharatha Natyam*, my engagement with the text tried to reconcile what *Natyasastra* said about *natya* as well as the form and experience of *Bharatha Natyam*. This chapter elucidates the perspective of a contemporary Indian dancer looking back at relevant chapters of *Natyasastra* and expanding the material in the light of her practice and experience of *Bharatha Natyam*.

Dance as Authentic Movement

As an experienced dancer, my journey to the texts came after intense immersion in the practice of *Bharatha Natyam*. I read about the rules of dancing only after I had learned the rudiments of *Bharatha Natyam* and practiced it for over 25 years. I reviewed texts to better understand and explain my own experience of dancing. The *Natyasastra* affirmed that while my experience of dancing was personal and unique, the evocation of such as experience was central to *natya*. It validated my experience as consistent with the premise of *natya*.

I was curious to know how other dancers experienced their dancing. This led me to the works of dancers such as Anna Halprin, Mary Whitehouse, Marion Chace, and several others. I stumbled upon a treasure trove of writings on dance as an authentic self-expression. For example, Anna Halprin's lifelong engagement with dance had led her to state that dancing uncovered long forgotten emotions that reside deep inside the body and she uses movement to express and release these feelings (2000, pp. 20–29). She also questioned the separation between the 'embodied' dancer who was the performer and the 'detached' observer was the disembodied spectator (Ross, 2007, p. 242). Halprin's work included the active engagement of audience and co-creation of an active performer—audience relationship (Ross, 2007, p. 230).

I resonated with her described experience of dancing, her identified participation of an engaged audience. However, I felt

73

differently about dancing being an expression of our personal emotions, from recent or distant past. While dancing some emotions, I sensed that my own personal experiences sometimes tempered the depiction. However when it came to my experience of the character (distinct from its depiction and portrayal), I could not correlate it with my personal life experience.

Additionally, Halprin's work suggested freedom from structure and stepping away from dancing form in order to experience authenticity of dance. The emphasis was on allowing the emotions to emerge and manifest as movements of the body— inviting the dance to move a dancer's body. The suggestion appeared to be that adherence to technique and form may impede the expression and experience of authentic dancing. This conflicted with my experience of *Bharatha Natyam* where its stylized and complex form somehow facilitated an authentic emotional experience. While I resonated with the experience of oneness in dancing that Halprin described, the language of authentic and free movements was not inclusive of the form and structure in *Bharatha Natyam*. It affirmed that dancers from other styles of dancing also experienced a similar state of oneness in their dance, but did not provide me additional language on how the form of *Bharatha Natyam* may evoke its experience.

Dance as Healing Art

Several world dancers use dance and movement as a therapeutic practice, where emphasis shifted away from form and structure to its healing experience (Levy, 1992, p. 5). In the United States, three main pioneers emerged on the East Coast (Marian Chace, Blanche Evans, Lilijan Espenak) and three on the West Coast (Mary Whitehouse, Trudi Schoop, Alma Hawkins), with a later emergence in the Mid-West (Franziska Boas, Elizabeth Rosen)—each with a distinctive approach to dance therapy (Levy, 1992, p. 23). Chace used dance to communicate and interact with people diagnosed with schizophrenia, who were harder to "reach" (Chace, Chaiklin & Sandel, 1993). Evans focused on drawing out creativity in the "neurotic urban Adult" and emphasized physical posture in using the body as an instrument of dance (Levy, 1992, p. 33). Espenak combined improvisation with structure as a way to project emotion; Schoop believed that miming in dance was a way to externalize inner conflicts; Hawkins helped people find their "authentic" movement to integrate mind and body; and, Boas used music and sound as auditory guides to elicit body's organic responses (Levy, 1992).

As a psychotherapist, I believed their experiences were powerful and authentic. I had personally seen the effect of movement and music on client's mood and emotional state. I agreed with their experience that dance is a way to balance internal energies and find a harmony within the body. However, their work suggested that the energy behind the experience of dancing came from within the dancer and dancing was the manner in which this integration came about. While I agreed that dancing facilitated this integration, I was not convinced that the energy came entirely from within the dancer.

My experience of *Bharatha Natyam* included the physical form and structure of this style of dance that facilitated its experience. My experience of *Bharatha Natyam* included the 'I' that experienced dancing. However, the emotional energy that permeated a dancer's body is suggestive of multiple resources with an internal experience of harmony. For instance, the presence and energetic engagement of audience enhanced the emotional experience of the dancer. Similarly, if music was live accompaniment to dance, I wondered about the energetic enhancement and contribution of such an engaged musician or musicians. I wondered if the harmony itself is purely internal or if it is an experience that is internal, suggestive of both internal and external energy. I wondered if the emotional energy of dancing reflected the collaborative and combined energies of many.

Apollonian and Dionysian Dance

Mary Starks Whitehouse articulated that for her, dance at "its ideal moment in time" was a coming together of "moving and being moved" (Pallaro, 1999, p. 47); it was "finding movement"

75

within the body which then allowed for experiences to present themselves (1999, pp. 53–54). She gave voice to her inner conflict between form and improvisation that turned into Tao, a way, a becoming (1999, pp. 60–62). In many ways, Whitehouse's conflict was also mine—an Apollonian and Dionysian struggle. On one hand, I was drawn to the purity of the experience that is embodied in dancing. And on the other, I sought a conceptual framework to understand and hold this experience. I dance within the form of *Bharatha Natyam*, enveloped and overwhelmed by its experience. And this study develops a language that holds both aspects in an integrated conceptual framework.

Which Comes First?

As I critically inquired about my own experiences, I questioned if it would apply to other dancers. I wondered if my experience has more to do with my personality and who I am, and less to do with dancing. However, reading about other dancer's experience suggested that this may be a commonality between dancers, even when trained in different styles of dancing. And it was also possible that dance somehow honed the inherent skill in individuals that allowed for such experiences.

While developing a suitable method for this study, I wondered if I could really suggest that *Bharatha Natyam* is Natya Yoga as an unequivocal statement. I wondered if my dance was simply an expression of 'me' and my experience of 'me' was entirely unique to me. Was it possible that 'I' was a Yogi and dance was reflecting this aspect of my self. However, what if it was my practice of *Bharatha Natyam* that created this aspect of 'me'?

It may be difficult to determine which entity is a prerequisite—is it the dancer's inherent ability to experience dancing beyond its physical realm, or is it the power of dance to create this ability in a dancer. I wondered if it may well be a co-emergent arising of both, within the dance.

Experience in Indian Dance

As I searched for written documentation of experiences in Indian dance, I found that much of the writings dealt with techniques, such as those outlined in *Natyasastra*. The commentaries and interpretations described the rules for dance and techniques to be followed. However, there was minimal (tending to none) literature on the dancing experience itself, and especially in the context of Indian dance, and *Bharatha Natyam*.

It was essential for my study to create a text on a dancer's experience of dancing, so as to provide a reference point for my experience and understanding of *rasa*. The paucity of such written descriptions of *rasa* may speak to the inherent difficulty in describing experiences that by definition are to be experienced in order to be understood. Another factor with regards to literature on Indian dance may be that it is uncommon to find dancers who are also scholars dedicated to writing about their dance. With the exception of a select few such as Vatsyayan, many of the commentators on *Natyasastra* were scholars who were perhaps not dancers. This may have also contributed to any distance between the theoretical concepts of *Natyasastra* and the practice of *natya* and in this instance, *Bharatha Natyam*.

Un-Bracketing Expectations

As I entered the hermeneutic engagement with *Natyasastra* texts, my expectations were that I will find a framework that helps explain the connection between *natya* and *rasa*—the ability to create intense experiences while staying true to form and structure of dance. My expectations were that I will understand what sets *Bharatha Natyam* apart from other dances, in a manner which facilitates authentic experience, even while stylized in movements and restricted by clear rules on techniques. In order to understand the correlation between movement and experience in *Bharatha Natyam*, I studied the *Natyasastra* with diligence, to emphasize any underrepresented wisdom on the interconnectedness of movement and emotions; between form and its experience. My entry point had been the *Abhinaya Darpana* which was in some ways an abridged version of *Natyasastra* with dedicated focus on essential dancing techniques.

Abhinaya Darpana - Mirror of Gestures

Nandikesvara's *Abhinaya Darpana* written around 1000 CE was a text devoted to dancing, and based on Bharatha's *Natyasastra* (Ghosh, 1981). In 1917, Coomaraswamy translated into English a Telugu interpretation of *Abhinaya Darpana* that was written by Tiruvenkatachari in 1874 (Coomaraswamy & Duggirala, 1987). Ghosh stated that when he read Coomaraswamy's book, titled *The Mirror of Gestures*, he felt the need to study the *Natyasastra* in order to better comprehend the essence of *Abhinaya Darpana* (Ghosh, 1981). At the time since there were no available commentaries or translations of the *Natyasastra,* it was only in 1944 that he was able to complete his translation and commentary on *Abhinaya Darpana*, after about 20 years of work on it (Ghosh, 1981).

The *Abhinaya Darpana* presently used is reconstructed from five manuscripts, of which only two were complete. As it is often the case with historical texts, there was a disparity between the two later versions (Ghosh, 1981, p. 1). Nevertheless, there seems to be concurrence on many crucial descriptions. For example, *natya* means "to dance" especially as an expressive and rhythmic "shewing" (Coomaraswamy, 1987, p. 5). It is dramatized dancing—where it is the action and not the actor which is essential to the dramatic art (Coomaraswamy, 1987, p. 3). The *Abhinaya Darpana* emphasized the need for a dancer to step into the role of the character being portrayed. The playwright's focus was on writing suggestive words and poems, with the sole purpose of evoking *rasa* in the spectator (Ghosh, 1981, p. 6).

The major contribution of *Abhinaya Darpana* was the extensive detailing of hand gestures, also documented in the *Natyasastra*. When used in movement, they were called *nritta hasta* and did not serve an expressive purpose. When the same gesture was used to convey a mood (*bhava*) along with facial expression (*abhinaya*) the dance became expressive and was called *nritya*.

Rock - Paper - Scissor

There are twenty four hasta mudra described using single hand to convey specific meanings. For ease of understanding, if we recollect a game played by children where each participant holds their hand to symbolize either a rock, paper or scissors—these three hand positions would be *musti, pataka,* and *kartarimukha hasta mudra*. Musti is described in form as "the four fingers are bent into the palm, and the thumb set on them" (Coomaraswamy, 1987, p. 30). Pataka (flag) is when "the thumb is bent to touch the fingers, and the fingers are extended" (Ghosh, 1981, p. 49). Later commentaries illustrated how this would appear, possibly synthesizing practical knowledge and observing use by dancers. However, such artistic depictions of *hasta mudra* were later additions to the original texts. As such there are several *hasta* descriptions that do not match their practice in dance. For example, the *hasta* of *kartarimukha* (arrow shaft face) is while holding the *pataka* hasta with bent ring finger, "the forefinger and the little finger are outspread" (Coomaraswamy, 1987, p. 28). However in practice, *kartarimukha* is held as if to show scissors in their clipping motion—similar to the hand position used in the game previously referred. If I were to use words to describe it, *kartarimukha* is while holding a *pataka hasta,* bending the ring and little fingers to the palm and wrapping the thumb around them—stretching out the forefinger and pushing the extended middle finger inward. The image used in Coomaraswamy's book for this *hasta* was from a museum in Madras and depicted the hand per the description in *Abhinaya Darpana*. As a brief aside, this aspect of artistic illustration is seen in iconographic depictions that are interwoven into Indian architecture. The beauty of dancing images carved into stone act as illustrative history of dance. It also invites the suggestion that the language of dance may be better captured in artistic depictions, either illustrations, photographs or as in this study by a video documentation.

When it comes to the twenty three double hand gestures, these gestures make sense only when both hands are used. For example, *anjali* (salutation) is when "two *pataka* hands are joined palm to palm" (Ghosh, 1981, p. 39). The *Abhinaya Darpana* described *hasta* to depict planets, animals, specific gods, and to show relationships (for example husband, wife, brother, etc.) (Ghosh, 1981, pp. 44 –51). Each of the *hasta* also have suggestive meanings, such as *musti* can be used to suggest steadiness, grasping hair, holding things, wrestling, etc. (Coomaraswamy, 1987 p. 30). Considering the suggestive uses of *kartarimukha*, it can be used to depict separation, confluence, eyes, a vine, etc. As a dancer, it occurs to me that holding my hand as described in the text is not as suggestive of an eye, as is using *kartarimukha* in the manner it is presently practiced. Perhaps, over time, dancers modified the original *hasta* to better serve the purpose of expressive communication.

Abhinaya Darpana described head positions and movements with suggestions on their use to express meanings. For instance, the text described a head movement called *duta* that was moving the head side to side as if to say 'no' or in denial or even to express astonishment (Coomaraswamy, 1987, pp. 18–19). Even while there were numerous uses prescribed for each defined part of the body, the dancer was also given discretion to create anew or modify what existed to better serve the larger purpose of evoking a particular rasa.

The *Abhinaya Darpana* stated that "Where the hand goes the eyes should follow, where the eyes go the mind follows, where the mind goes emotion arises, when there is emotion *rasa* is evoked" (Coomaraswamy, 1987, p. 17). However, the *Abhinaya Darpana* did not provide any further details on *rasa*. When discussing expressions of an emotion, a*bhinaya* (expression) is described as suggestive imitation of an emotion; and Ghosh suggests that when there is such an enactment in speech and gesture, this evoked in the spectator, impressions of emotions drawn from their own experiences—this produced an experience (*rasa*) in them (1981, p. 6). For example, sorrow is depicted with *duta* head movement along with the appropriate expressive eyes, in this case *visanna* eye movement (Ghosh, 1981, p. 11). A receptive spectator is reminded of their own personal experience, which then triggers within a re-experience or recollection of the emotions of that experience. While this may apply to some audience members, I was not entirely convinced that personal experience was a prerequisite to experiencing a dancer's portrayed emotion. And more relevant to this study, the text does not give voice to the dancer's experience of dancing.

Missing pieces

The *Abhinaya Darpana* described how various parts of the body can be used in depicting and expressing emotions. It did not discuss the use of facial expressions, or emotional states of various characters being depicted, or role of music in dance. While there was reiteration that the ultimate goal in dancing is the experience of *rasa*, the *Abhinaya Darpana* did not focus on this aspect adequately.

As related to my study, this gap precipitated the need for further reading, starting with a deeper engagement with the *Natyasastra*. As I reviewed the *Natyasastra*, the scope and magnitude of what could be said seems immense. For the purposes of this study, my intent is not to offer a translation or interpretation or commentary of this seminal work. My interest is in deep engagement with specific portions of the text that speak to the experience of dancing—such as the chapters on *bhava*(emotion), *abhinaya*(expression), *rasa*(experience), and *natya*(dancing). However, I intend to provide the context in which these chapters are situated within the *Natyasastra*.

While writing about my engagement, I am conscious not to overwhelm reader with technical Sanskrit terms that are not entirely relevant or significant to my study. At the same time, I am aware of the necessity in finding an appropriate depth of analysis that is evident in my writing.

Natyasastra

The eminence of *Natyasastra* stems from the fact that it was the first comprehensive treatise on Indian dramaturgy even though it was not necessarily the first on the subject (Rangacharya, 1986, p. ix). It acts as a "single cohesive fountainhead for all arts" (Indian)—principally for theater, including poetry, dance, music, architecture, etc. (Vatsyayan, 1996, p. 26). The *Natyasastra* has 36 chapters dedicated to topics such as the techniques of dance and drama, rules for architecture of dance hall, musical composition, types of dramatic presentations, ideal qualities of a dancer-dramatist and an overview of the place of *natya* in Indian society (Ghosh, 1967). The text comes down to us in *Prakrit*, and is slightly different from *Sanskrit* (Vatsyayan, 1996, p. 17). The *Natyasastra* is considered to be the most comprehensive treatise on artistic expression and methodologies for evoking response and resonance in the audience (Vatsyayan, 1996, p. 53). However, a criticism has been made that its author, Bharatha considered only the most cultivated styles while considering the rules that would apply universally to effective dramatic presentation; he did not include regional or popular varieties of dance and drama (Bose, 2007, p. 2).

Bharatha

It is speculated by commentators such as Ghosh, Vatsyayan, and Rangacharya that Bharatha must have been privy to a wide range of drama presentations. He was able to distill from them the attributes that rendered them effective and successful in communicating with the audience. He then compiled his observations into rules, techniques and guidelines to follow when composing and presenting drama. However, he also consciously created it as a fluid text—stating that practitioners could change these rules according to the needs of time and place (Kumar, 2006, p. xxi). The efficacy of the *Natyasastra* lies in the emergence of multiple forms of practice (*prayoga*) in Indian dance that embody the fluidity of rules (*sastra*) that are codified in it. It is therefore also referred to as a *prayoga sastra* or theory of practice / practice of theory (Vatsyayan, 1996, p. 38).

Dating the Text

The *Natyasastra* is dated between second century BCE and second century CE (Kumar, 2006, p. xvi). Considering that this work was compiled so many hundreds of years ago, a valid question is about its authorship. How do we know that one author wrote it? There is speculation that Bharatha compiled verses that were present, integrating them into his writings and created one comprehensive text in the Natyasastra. For instance, within the text of *Natyasastra*, Bharatha quotes some verses set in a different rhythmic meter, and also attributes it to previous authors (Rangacharya, 1986, p. 43). Bhat writes that *Natyasastra* must have grown out of the original *Nata Sutra* (1975, p. iii). Also, Rangacharya and Ghosh among several commentators, propose that the word *bharata* (referring to an actor) may suggest that the *Natyasastra* is for *bharata* (actors) and not necessarily by Bharatha. However, while the writing shows complexities and is at times sequentially out of order, there are no contradictions. This demonstrates unity of purpose suggesting an integrated vision of a single author (Vatsyayan, 1996, p. 6). At present, the *Natyasastra* is recognized as the work of Bharatha, and may also include original writings by previous scholars.

Incomplete manuscripts of the *Natyasastra* were available in India between twelfth and eighteenth century CE (Kumar, 2006, p. xx). Other commentaries on the *Natyasastra* were by Udbhata in seventh century, Lollata in mid-eighth century, Sankuka in 813 CE, Kirtidhara in ninth or tenth century CE and Abhinavagupta in eleventh century CE (Rangacharya, 1986, p. xii). The last two authors also refer to commentaries by Bhattayantra and Bhattanayaka. Among all these commentaries, Abhinavagupta's work is the only commentary on *Natyasastra* that is available. He called the elaborate elucidation of the rules of *natya* as *Natya-veda-vivrti* although it is commonly referred to as *Abhinavabharati* (Deshpande, 1989, p. 25). The *Abhinavabharati* was discovered in a Southern Indian state of Kerala, between 1900 and 1926 (Kumar, 2006, p. xix). The commentary was missing portions of text, notably from the fourth verse in Chapter 7 through the end of Chapter 8 (Shah, 2003, p. 69). Chapter 6 in *Natyasastra* and Abhinavabharati deals with *rasa* (experience), chapter 7 with *bhava* (emotion) and chapter 8 with *abhinaya* (expression). There are no available commentaries on chapter 8 of the *Natyasastra* (Bose, 2007, p. 22). The text of *Natyasastra* used at present is a synthesis of incomplete and complete manuscripts of *Natyasastra* and *Abhinavabharati* (Vatsyayan, 1996, p. 29).

Abhinavagupta's understanding of *Natyasastra* led to his suggestion that the purpose of *natya* was to evoke *rasa*. However, the relevant chapters that discuss the emotional experience and its expression in dancing are incompletely available to us. We are not given textual support that provides elaboration on what led Abhinavagupta to his understanding of *natya*. We have other allied writings by Abhinavagupta that suggest his philosophical perspectives may have been influenced by Kashmir Saivism. However, this gap in *Natyasastra* literature on the interconnectedness of emotion—expression—experience (*bhava—abhinaya—rasa*) is central to this study. I wonder if there was a written description of a connection between the form of *natya* (*abhinaya*) and its experience in *rasa* that we may have lost over time.

Perspectives

Vatsyayan comments that especially when describing the aesthetic experience of dance, commentators have approached their interpretation of *Natyasastra*, from different systems of Indian philosophy viz. *nyaya, sankhya, Vedanta, or Kashmira Saivism* (1968, p. 7). While it may be of interest to study each of these viewpoints and authors, for the purpose of this study emphasis is placed on Abhinavagupta, whose work has largely informed the composition and understanding of *Natyasastra*.

Abhinavagupta lived between 965 and 1025 CE based on his other written works (Pande, 1997, p. 3). His literary activities seem to have lasted for 25 years between 990 and 1015 CE (Deshpande, 1989, p. 23). He is described as a scholar, poet, critic, musician, saint and philosopher who studied *Natyasastra* and its literary criticism from Bhatta Tauta (Pande, 1997, p. 4) Abhinavagupta collected and expounded Saiva Agamic traditions of Kashmir, giving them a systematic philosophic form, wrote about doctrines of resonance (*dvani)* and the experiential concept of *rasa* in light of philosophy of Kashmir Saivism (Pande, 1997, p. 4).

Natya Veda

The *Natyasastra* narrates the story of its creation, as its introduction. Since the existing four *veda (Rig* Veda, *Sama Veda, Yajur Veda* and *Atharvana Veda)* had become inaccessible to much of the population, the creator of the universe, Brahma, after deep meditation, created a fifth *veda* called *Natya Veda.* Rangacharya wrote that the dictates of these four *veda* were no longer effective in serving as guidelines for righteous living and people are described as being consumed by greed, avarice, jealousy, and anger (1986). So, in order to help overcome unpleasant emotions, the *Natya Veda* was created to teach people while pleasing "eyes and ears" (Rangacharya, 1986, p. 3).

Brahma created the *Natya Veda* by integrating the essence of the existing four *veda* and incorporated all arts and sciences in the fifth *Natya Veda* (Shah, 2003, p. 91). He took the concept of words from *Rig Veda,* the essence of music from *Sama Veda,* ideas on movements and make up from *Yajur Veda,* and those on emotional acting from *Atharvana Veda.* When the gods were asked to practice this form, Indra (king of the gods) asks that only sages could practice it, as the dictates of *Natya Veda* state that the ideal practitioners are those who are smart, intelligent, observant, possess knowledge in *veda* and can exercise self-control (Rangacharya, 1986). And so, Bharatha is asked to teach and spread this form of *natya veda* among those who are worthy of practicing it.

The practice of this art form is to induce (in audience) a temporary state of "forgetfulness" and provide escape into the world of happiness (Bhat, 1975, p. ix). Witnessing such a *natya* is comparable to mastery of *veda,* performing sacrifices or generous giving of gifts (Vatsyayan, 1996, p. 11). The *Natyasastra* states that *natya* represents the actions and feelings of all and it brings peace, entertainment and happiness to the viewer. It is emphatically stated that there is no art, no knowledge, no yoga, no action that is not found in *natya* (Rangacharya, 1986, p. 5). Indian poets and playwrights often include a benediction of universal prosperity as a result of reading or listening to their words. I have danced to where the poet writes that "listening to this devotional song will ensure good health and prosperity for several generations." I have danced historical stories that describe the spiritual benefits of *natya* in worship and community prayer. It is also my personal bias that *natya* is an integrated experience of the physical, emotional and spiritual aspects of life. This study works to develop transdisciplinary vocabulary that can better language such a comprehensive human experience that is *natya*.

Natya and Rasa

The *Natyasastra* states *natya* is when an actor does not "act a role," portray a character, imitate, or "pretend" to feel an emotion; it is when the actor "dance(s)" the character (Ghosh, 1967). The dancer-actor has to step into the experience of the character. The *Natyasastra* describes the form of *natya* that facilitates the dancer's entry into the experiential world of the character.

The *Natyasastra* provides a descriptive manual on the techniques of *natya*. It describes the multiplicity of aesthetic experiences—nine types of emotional experience (*nava rasa*). It suggests a connection between each emotion (*bhava)* and its corresponding experience (rasa). It describes how specific emotions (*bhava*) are depicted by the dancer. The descriptions create a visual image of how the dancer appears when enacting each emotion as the character. The *Natyasastra* describes the role of facial expressions in conveying an authentic experience of the character. It suggests how subtle movements can convey the character's emotional state of being. It describes how the body is held (hands, feet, arms, eyes, etc.) in such portrayal.

When describing the physical space where *natya* is to be performed, the *Natyasastra* provides great deal of detail on the structural dimensions of the dance hall, the sculptural representations of various deities to guard the hall and rituals to initiate a performance. The selection of appropriate dancers to suit the character, their attire and accessories that convey the personality of a character, and even the physical attributes of an ideal dancer are described in the *Natyasastra*. The significance of music is represented by its emphasis on variety of musical instruments to be used, the rhythmic permutations to be followed, and the lyrical composition of songs, poems and speech spoken by the character. The role of a dancer includes dancing, singing, speaking, acting and other actions that co-create a successful, dramatic presentation.

Natya includes dance, drama, and music (Rangacharya, 1986, p. 3). *Natya* refers to dramatic dancing, governed by the dictates of the *Natyasastra*. The practitioners of *natya*, while possessing "power, knowledge and skill" is not "arrogant, egoistic" and instead should have "discipline, self-restraint, self-transcendence, and humility" (Kumar, 2006, p. xii). The dancer's "subjective personal experience" plays no part in the artistic creation and re-creation of aesthetic experience in the spectator (Vatsyayan, 1968, p. 4). Talking with Dr. Kapila Vatsyayan (personal meeting, November 8, 2011), she explained that her lifelong practice of dancing had privileged her with a dancer's view and understanding of the *Natyasastra*. While *Natyasastra* is a book of rules and techniques, rules can be fully appreciated only when there is a realization of the "greater purpose and function" they serve (Vatsyayan, 1968, p. 9).

The suggestion is that a dancer's reality in dancing the character is not shaped by personal life experience. While dance is an expression of self, the emotional energy of this expression may be a manifestation of intermingling of multiple sources such as the conducive dancing space, presence of an engaged audience, vitality of a dancer, vibrancy of music, etc.

Bharatha states that without *rasa* there can be no dramatic depiction (Shah, 2003, p. 91). Vatsyayan states that Bharatha's "sole aim" in *Natyasastra* was to describe techniques by which a particular *rasa* could be evoked (1968, p. 9). Abhinavagupta defines *natya* as the "intuitive experience of *rasa*" (Pande, 1997, p. 17). Interpretations of *Natyasastra* indicate that evoking an experience of *natya* was its primary if not main purpose. It validates my experience that *natya* and Indian dancing was more than beautiful body movements. The audience's participative engagement and experience of *natya* somehow contributed to the phenomenology of dancing. The form of *natya* played a role in somehow facilitating its experience. The next section explores this connection between movement (*nritta*) and expressive dance (*nritya* and *natya*).

Nritta - Nritya - Natya

The Natyasastra states that pure movements (*nritta*) of the body carry no "meaning" and their significance is in the creation of beauty in dance (Bose, 2007, p. 116). *Natya*, by contrast is expressive for the sole purpose of creating *rasa* (aesthetic experience) in audience (Rangacharya, 1986, p. 38). Around the tenth century CE, a third concept of dancing called *nritya* was first mentioned by Dhananjaya in his compilation of ten types of plays titled, *Dasarupaka* (Bose, 2007). He described *nritya* as a combination of *nritta* and *natya* that incorporates the element of movement from *nritta* and the purpose of emotional expression of *natya* (Bose, 2007). While the format of *natya* is in the context of a dramatized play, *nritya* pertains to expressive dancing without a larger story that is narrated in a play. While *natya* includes vocalized expressions of scripted speech, singing, expressive dancing, interpretive storytelling, stylized costumes, accessories, masks and face paints and other forms of dramatic expressions, *nritya* is expression that is contained to the medium of dance. In many ways, *nritya* is the aspect of *natya* that is embodied in the form of dance.

However, neither Bharatha nor Abhinavagupta use the term *nritya* to refer to dancing (Bose, 2007, p. 22). It was much later, around thirteenth century CE, *nritya* became dissociated from *natya* and used exclusively for the art of dancing— *Sangitaratnakara* (a text on music by Sarangadeva) defines *nritya* categorically as dance for the first time (Bose, 2007, p. 169). In the context of *Bharatha Natyam* as a dance form, the aspect of drama or play is less common. The aspects of *natya* that are used in *Bharatha Natyam* are also consistent with the description of *nritya*. However in this study, the word *natya* is used to refer to dancing and includes movement (*nritta*) and expressive storytelling (*nritya*).

Nritta

After preliminary benedictions and introduction of *natya* as the fifth *veda*, chapter four of *Natyasastra* describes *tandava* (energetic, dynamic, vigorous) dance movements. This chapter describes that when Bharatha presented the first choreographed drama to Siva, recognized as the God of Indian dance, the latter contributed *karana* (synchronized movement), *angahara* (sequential movement) and hand gestures. *Karana* are described as synchronized movement of hands and feet to achieve a prescribed range of movement (Rangacharya, 1986, p. 18). There are 108 *karana* described in the *Natyasastra*. For example, *Samanakha* is defined as "the two feet touching each other toe to toe the two hands hanging down and the body in a natural (straight) pose" (Rangacharya, 1986, p. 19). While *karana* are occasionally misinterpreted as static poses, they are really cadences of movement (Subrahmanyam, n.d.) For example, *Viksipta* is described as "hand and foot thrown out together to the side or backwards" (Rangacharya, 1986, p. 21). While movement is implied in reaching such a position, often times *karana* represented as a stationary pose, whereas it may only be suggestive of the range of movement. In some ways, *karana* may serve the equivalent of a picture where the dancer holds the position to be captured. However, the dancing aspect is in moving into that position, holding it for an appropriate length of time and moving out of it and into the next position.

The most common depictions of *karana* are sculptural on the walls of temples and courtyards. Many of the *karana* have accompanying hand positions and precise form. When several (up to nine) *karana* are combined sequentially, it is called an *angahara*. For both *karana* and *angahara*, basic units of feet position, leg and body posture, hand gestures, eye movements, etc. interact as prescribed. In present day *Bharatha Natyam*, the combination of movements referred to as ad*avu* are the closest representation of *karana* (and *angahara*) (Vatsyayan, 1974, p. 25). Several such *adavu* are sequentially danced to rhythm and/or melodic music. The body movements in *Bharatha Natyam* are rhythmic and graceful without interpretive significance and are referred to as *nritta*.

When Siva contributed his dynamic and vigorous *Tandava* dance, his consort Parvathi who stood by watching him was inspired to dance similar movements (*sukumaraprayoga*), except with a delicacy and grace that distinguished it in style of dancing and not its substance (Bose, 2007, p. 116).This style was termed *lasya,* an expressive dance created from delicate body movements (Bose, 2007, p. 15). *Tandava* and *lasya* movements are occasionally represented as different kinds of dance movements. It is important to note that they are simply different ways of expressing the same or similar movements. While the vocabulary of movement may be similar, their language and manner of expression distinguishes them as dynamic (*tandava*) and graceful (*lasya*), both of which are attributes of *nritta*.

Hand gestures that do not serve an expressive function are called *nritta hasta* and while prescribed for *karana*, *hasta mudra* were only described in later Chapters 9 and 10. This is one of the several inexplicable complexities noted by commentators of *Natyasastra* (Rangacharya, 1986). There are *hasta mudra* described for use by a single hand and when used to form a gesture together. Each mudra is described in form and also in its expressive uses. This aspect of *hasta mudra* is described with great detail in the *Abhinaya Darpana* that was discussed earlier in this book.

The use of the physical body in movement is described through concepts of *nritta, tandava, karana, angahara, cari* (moving only one leg), and *recaka* (term referring to body movements) of various parts of the body. The integrated use of feet in posture and movement, along with arms and hand gestures, combined with eye glances represented the movement aspect (*nritta*) of *natya* which was reiterated as not having an interpretive purpose, but one that creates visual beauty for the spectator.

Bhava - Abhinaya - Rasa

Chapter 6 of the *Natyasastra* deals with *rasa* and states unequivocally that *rasa* is the cumulative result of a stimulus (*vibhava*), its involuntary reaction (*anubhava*), and voluntary action (*vyabhicaribhava)* (Rangacharya, 1986, p. 38). "That which conveys the meaning intended by the poet through words, physical gestures and facial changes is a b*hava*" (Rangacharya, 1986, p. 44). *Vibhava* is that which leads to perception—it is the cause (of reaction and action) (Rangacharya, 1986, p. 44).

When a stimulus triggers a response, it becomes a determinant for that reaction. This determinant is called *vibhava*. The reaction that is spontaneous, involuntary, and reactive is called *anubhava*. For example, if the *vibhava* is mimicking another's action, its corresponding *anubhava* may be a smile or even laughter. If the *vibhava* is the death of a loved one, its corresponding *anubhava* may be tears and crying (Kumar, 2006, p. 281).

The expression or action that is deliberate, deeper, and considered is called *vyabhicaribhava*. For example, if the stimulus or determinant or *vibhava* is absence of a beloved, the consequent or involuntary reaction or *anubhava* may be feeling lonely and missing their presence. The action *or vyabhicaribhava* (also called *sancari bhava)* could be writing a letter to express loneliness, or crying in desperation or becoming angered, while suspecting infidelity.

How a character acts is also dependent on the personality and emotional state *(sthayibhava).* Of the eight personality types *(ashta nayika)* of heroines, one who is angry *(kandita)* at her lover's absence may fight with him when he does come. A heroine who is pining in separation *(proshitabhartrka)* may cry while waiting patiently for his arrival. A heroine who is assertive *(abhisarika)* may leave in search of him, without waiting for his action. The *sthayibhava* (eight in number) are love, humor, compassion, horror, heroic, fear, repulsion and wonder.

The *sthayibhava* of the character being portrayed is the dominant emotion *(bhava)* that influences how the character responds to a stimulus (Rangacharya, 1986, p. 45). A character whose *sthayi* is love, while in the company of her beloved *(vibhava),* may react *(anubhava)* with sweet words and loving glances with her eyes (Kumar, 2006, p. 252). In depicting this *bhava* the dancer incorporates as described in the *Natyasastra* the prescribed techniques for eyes, eyebrows, lips, head, *hasta mudra,* feet position, etc. so as to convey the emotion *(bhava)* of love. When this emotion of love is also experienced by the audience, it is called *rasa* and the *rasa* of love is called *sringara rasa.*

The act and technique of such expression is called *abhinaya* and is of 4 kinds—spoken *(vacika),* physical body *(angika),* accessories *(aharya)* and emotional *(satvika)* (Rangacharya,1986, p. 53). The *Natyasastra* describes how a character whose *sthayi* is anger should be dressed—the costume colors that convey anger, masks that depict an angry person, the type of rhythmic permutation that expresses the energy of anger, and so on. The experience of anger is the fourth type of *abhinaya* (expression) called *satvika abhinaya.* While the other types of expression create a visual image of what an angry character looks like, there is not a comparable description of what the character feels much less how a dancer can step into the experiential world of such a character.

Bhava (emotion) is understood as provocation (*vibhava*), reaction (*anubhava*), and action (*sancaribhava* / *vyabhicaribhava*) - all of which are informed by the emotional state (*sthayibhava*) of the character. Another aspect of *bhava* is *satvika bhava* which is an experience of the realistic emotion of the character. When a dancer is able to step into the experiential world of a character, the dancer experiences the emotional state (*sthayi*) of the character. This authentic experience of the *sthayi* is called *satvika bhava* of the emotion. The authenticity of this emotion is then conveyed to the audience through *satvika abhinaya*, a genuine and spontaneous expression of the emotional experience of the character's personality and emotional state. The audience can see, hear, sense and feel the emotional experience of the character being portrayed. This emotional and aesthetic experience by the spectator is *rasa* (Rangacharya, 1986, p. 44). The latent emotional state called *sthayibhava* when energized and expressed through appropriate and authentic *abhinaya*, evokes the corresponding *rasa* in the audience. When the *bhava* (emotion) is compassion, the *sthayi* is compassion, its corresponding *rasa* is the experience of compassion, also called *karuna rasa*.

For the eight sthayibhava there are eight corresponding *rasa—sringara* (love), *hasya* (humor), *karuna* (compassion), *raudra* (terror), *vira* (heroic), *bhayanaka* (fear), *bibhatsa* (repulsion), and ad*bhuta* (wonder). (Rangacharya, 1986, p. 37). *Sringara* is the experience(*rasa*) of love, *karuna* is the experience of compassion, *bhayanaka* is the emotional experience of fear, and ad*bhuta* is an experience of wonder. *Rasa* is the experience of the *sthayibhava* of a character, conveyed to the audience by a dancer who experiences the emotion that is expressed authentically.

The *Natyasastra* simply describes what each concept is and suggests their connection. For example, it describes the eight *sthayibhava* and the eight *rasa* with brief suggestion on how the two are related. If one were to read the *Natyasastra,* it may read as page after page of numerous terms of techniques, concepts and their confusing descriptions. The theory becomes relevant only with practice of dance, as is suggested by the author's description of the text as *prayoga sastra*—theory of practice/practice of theory (Vatsyayan, 1974, p. 25). As a stand alone text, *the Natyasastra* functions as a descriptive manual of dance terminology but not as an instruction manual for dancing. As such, while the descriptions include emotions and the nature of their experience, it does not instruct or suggest their practical connections, much less facilitation. This gap in language is what my study attempts to address. The study offers an expanded vocabulary that includes the form and experience of dancing, and the process inherent in its practice.

For the purpose of this discussion, I have integrated my experience as a dancer and presented a perspective on how these concepts connect practically in dance. As with subjective experiences, my understanding is based on my experiences and are not intended to speak for others, much less act as an interpretation of *Natyasastra*.

Since my engagement with texts followed my immersion in practice of *Bharatha Natyam*, I found that the vocabulary described in the *Natyasastra* useful to conceptualize and understand the interplay between action, reaction and emotion. The sequencing of *bhava* leading to *rasa* while described as discrete concepts was not immediately understood without the benefit of my experience of dancing. The explanations that I have offered are borne from my experience of dancing. This languaging of the words from *Natyasastra* is consistent with my experience of dancing.

Music in Dance

Dancing (*natya*) is to the accompaniment of instrumental music (*vadyam*) and vocal singing (*gitam*)—the interactions between these three is termed *sangita* (Shringy & Sharma, 2007, p. 10). In order to achieve an experience of integration and harmony, the *Natyasastra* prescribes a specific kind of music for natya—*Gandharva Sangita* which evokes *rasa* in its listeners (Gautam, 1993, p. 35). It describes the types of instruments to be used in *Gandharva Sangita* such as stringed, percussive and wind instruments (Rangacharya, 1986, p. 146). The text describes *vina* as an ideal string instrument and the flute as a wind instrument. *Gandharva Sangita* has three elements present—melody that is in a specific order or arrangement, rhythm, and suitable text (Gautam, 1993, p. 35). When the words are arranged in four lines, syllables become woven together to create a rhythmic meter (Rangacharya, 1986, p. 79).

Musical sequences are a combination of melodic notes in varying pitches composed to several rhythmic meters. Each of these permutations is categorized as a type or class (*jati*) and specific *jati* are prescribed to evoke a corresponding *rasa* (Rangacharya, 1986, pp. 149–151). Abhinavagupta describes *jati* as notes that are in a specific pattern that produce aesthetic enjoyment which also leads to "unseen spiritual benefits" (Gautam, 1993, p. 37). The melodic sequences are also referred to as *raga*—however, in the *Natyasastra* the word *raga* is used as "pleasure giving" rather than a technical term for melody (Gautam, 1993, p. 45). Similarly, when describing rhythm as *tala* and discussing the intervals, frequency and various techniques of keeping time, *Natyasastra* specifies *tala* that evokes corresponding *rasa* (Rangacharya, 1986, p. 165). The significance of *rasa* in music corresponds to its relevance in *natya*. The prescribed rhythmic combinations, melodic notes, instrument selection, lyrical content, etc. in music seem to share with *natya* the purpose of evoking *rasa* in the listener.

There are several chapters dedicated to rhythmic meter and structure in music; chapters that discuss the number of syllables to be used in a musical sequence; identification of various types of musicals; and, description of actors ideal for each musical role (Rangacharya, 1986). While *natya* includes the component of music, the interconnectedness between dancing, music and drama is suggestive. For the purpose of this study, dancing's dependence on music is not explored further, except to reiterate that *nritta* depends for its life breath on music and rhythm while *nritya* depends on the theme of the narrative of the song (Vatsyayan, 1968, p. 19).

My experience as a dancer has taught me the value of music that resonates with me. When a singer vocalizes the emotions inherent in the melody and lyrical content of the song, it invites me to step into the musical experience. It facilitates my entry and transition into the experiential world of the character. It holds space for the emotional expression in my dance. I wonder if emotional experience and expression in dance would be possible with the resonant music. I wonder if the dancer taps into the emotional energy of music and amplifies it in dancing. I wonder if dance is an integrated expression of music, audience, physical space and dancer—and if *rasa*, its reflective experience.

Where Does Rasa Reside?

My inquiry is into the dancer's experience of dance. My experience of dancing has included an immersion in dancing and an awareness of the immersion. Savoring of the experience has been in hindsight, looking back and reliving the immersion. The word *rasa* that is used in *Natyasastra* and its commentaries suggest an experience that is similar to relishing and enjoying its essence. This study emphasizes the momentary experience of *rasa* in dancing. However, to establish a firm grounding, this section undertakes a brief exploration into the how *rasa* has been described and understood in the context of Indian dance.

Appa Rao and Rama-Sastry believe that *rasa* "is a triumvirate experience shared equally by author, actor & sympathetic mind"

(1967, p. 19). External factors such as physical space, audience participation, caliber of music, etc. affect the experience of dancing. *Rasa* is sensitive to time and space. I believe that each person's experience is unique not only to that person, but also to that specific time and place. While many may experience *rasa* each experience is distinct, and I am unsure if it can be a "shared" experience.

According to Bhatta Lollata, *rasa* is in the character described; Sankuka stated it resides only in the actor; Bhattanayaka suggested it is only in the audience; Abhinavagupta after careful examination of all previous opinions stated categorically that *rasa* is the audience's experience (Appa Rao, 1967, pp. 26–27). If *rasa* is an individual experience, then each of the above statements may hold true. The character exists only in the mind of the playwright, in the experience of the actor and the audience. As such the character's experience may be synonymous with the actor's experience of *rasa*. Additionally if the expressive abilities of the actor do not match the ability to immerse in the experience of the character, the *rasa* enjoyed by the actor may not include the audience. However for the audience to experience *rasa*, it is necessary for the dancer/actor to express the emotion appropriately. Can a dancer express what is not experienced authentically? And can the right audience member experience an emotion that even the dancer does not feel? If the audience member is an actor/dancer and has developed the ability to sense emotions and resonate with the music and dance, their ability to experience *rasa* may not entirely depend on that particular dancer's ability to experience *rasa*. This introduces the concept of *sahrdaya*—one who is capable of experiencing *rasa*.

In any audience group, only some members have this ability to experience *rasa*. They are called *sahrdaya*—one who is capable of " self-transcendence" and resonance with an "universal experience of bliss" (Appa Rao, 1967, pp. 29–30). With prolonged exposure to *natya* and other arts, an engaged observer develops the ability to resonate with an emotional experience and expression. Such a sensitive person (*sahrdaya*) has an ability to sense and tune into the emotional energy that permeates a dancing hall.

The emotional experience (*rasa*) by a *sahrdaya* is likened to a mystical experience of the Absolute, *Brahman* (Vatsyayan, 1996, pp. 145–147). Similar but not identical to it, because *rasa* is "momentary and recollection is subsequent" (Vatsyayan, 1996, pp. 145–147). Vatsyayan touches upon the distinction between "immersion" and "awareness"—the awareness and recollection of the immersion in dance evokes *rasa* in the dancer. My curiosity is about the immersive moments (while somewhat aware) in dancing. If this is a prerequisite to *rasa*, what is the immersion called? In my dancing experience, it is being overwhelmed and immersed by an emotion that is intense, filled with joy and beauty, powerful and graceful.

The *rasa* that describes my immersive experience the best, is both *ananda* (joy) and *shanta* (tranquility). The *Natyasastra* does not describe either emotion as an experience (*rasa*). However, Abhinavagupta describes a ninth *rasa* called *shanta rasa*—while some consider it an addition to the eight described in the *Natyasastra,* others think of it as the basis for the experience of the eight (Raghavan, 1980,p. 98). Kalanidhi Narayanan, an experienced dancer and leading exponent of *abhinaya* writes that "Shanta—serenity—is a state of equanimity—different emotions are evoked from this state & it is to this state of inner tranquility that one reverts to in the end" (1994, p. 33). Abhinavagupta also described aesthetic experience at its highest level as an experience of self itself, as pure and mixed bliss (*maharasa* state) (Deshpande, 1989, p. 84).

Reviewing the *Natyasastra* and engaging with its interpretations and commentaries has introduced new vocabulary and also pointed out the gaps that still exist in my mind. I had entered this dance with the text to understand the phenomenology of dancing; I wanted to reconcile the textual material with my experience of *Bharatha Natyam*. The *Natyasastra* reiterates that there can be no *natya* without *rasa* (Rangacharya, 1986, p. 38).

Evoking an authentic experience of dancing is the purpose of natya. It validated my experience of dancing as consistent with the premise of *Bharatha Natyam*. My perspective changed to understanding how the numerous concepts and techniques described in the *Natyasastra* helped create *rasa*.

The descriptions of the techniques used in *nritta* (movement) included moving arms, hands, feet, legs, eyes, eyebrows among other body movements to rhythmic and melodic music. While *nritta* is graceful, swift, percussive and fluid in its beautiful form, I could not reconcile its relevance to *rasa*. The *Natyasastra* suggests that *nritta* has no interpretive purpose and yet describes its technique over several chapters. While it states that *natya* is to evoke *rasa*, it does not offer the connection between *nritta* and *rasa*. What is the relevance of movement to an experience of dancing? In some ways, I am left wondering about the relevance of form to experience.

The *Natyasastra* describes in detail the nuances of emotion (*bhava*), its expression (*abhinaya*) and its experience (*rasa*). It functions as a descriptive manual for these various concepts that make complete sense only with a practical experience of dancing. The *Natyasastra* does not function well as an instruction manual for dance. In keeping with its suggestive language, there is no clear direction on how a dancer is able to step into the experiential world of the character. There is no suggestion of a conceptual framework that holds together the form of dance (which is thoroughly described in the text) and connects with its experience.

While *Natyasastra* reiterates that *rasa* is the essence of *natya*, there is lack of clarity on whose *rasa*—the dancers or the audience. If *rasa* is the experience of the audience, what describes the experience of the dancer? There is suggestion that *rasa* experience (*rasa-vada*) is similar to mystical and spiritual experience. Is there another language that understands and describes *rasa differently?*

6. YOGASUTRA & ASHTA ANGA YOGA

Yogasutra is one of the earliest Indian texts that specifically described meditation as *dhyana*. The text outlined an eight-limbed system (*ashta anga*) in which the seventh is meditative immersion or *dhyana*. The *Yogasutra* also describes such immersion, as a step towards transcendence of physical self. With regards to this study, the eight principles (*ashta anga*) are studied with a view to expand the vocabulary to describe the experience of dancing. This chapter emphasizes how the form of a practice (such as *Bharatha Natyam*) can lead to an experience that transcends the physical self.

Situating Myself in The Study

The *Natyasastra* provides a strong grounding for the various techniques available to a dancer-dramatist. While it offers descriptions for movement (*nritta*) it does not suggest its relevance in creating *rasa*. However, the *Natyasastra* suggests that *rasa* is the purpose of *natya*. Since it does not discuss the process of creating *rasa*, much less any wisdom or reason for emphasizing its experience, this study explores the language of *Yogasutra* to understand how *rasa* may relate to mystical experience, as suggested by Abhinavagupta and Vatsyayan. Until the time of this study, I had not connected yoga with meditation. My initial impression of yoga was that it was a physical practice of postures and *asana* that developed flexibility in the body.

Interestingly enough, I had consciously practiced meditation by teaching my mind to quiet its thoughts, since I was about 20 years old. I resisted ritualistic and religious entry into practice of meditation. The various devotional verses did not attract me at the time. I did not understand how chanting words could be a meaningful spiritual exercise, especially words that I didn't comprehend much less resonate with. I wanted to connect with what religion refers to as God—and yet, systematized religious practices did not work for me. I learned to pray in a way that was authentic for me. I learned to be in the presence of a larger energy— something that was larger than my physical self. I had never doubted that there was such a presence. I found that I felt this presence best when I was not distracted by thoughts. I defaulted into learning how to quiet my thinking. I did not use a physical object to focus my attention on. It was instinctive and intuitive for me to sit at my mother's prayer altar and learn to just be in that space. Sometimes it was while she was performing rituals or reading devotional verses of prayer. It started as a few minutes and developed into longer and sustained periods of quiet mind time. I now recognize that this was/is a practice of meditation.

In my search for answers I explored several healing practices such as hypnosis, Reiki, Theta healing and other world traditions (indigenous) of accessing energy. Each system had a valid and credible entry point in working with inner and outer energies. However, it did not provide a conceptual framework to explain their process. Just when I had reached a point when I thought that perhaps there was no such satisfactory explanatory framework, yoga entered my life.

While I have always been a dancer, I don't consider myself dexterous enough to hold Yogic postures with my body. Dance has been my yoga practice. Everything I read about the theory and philosophy of yoga resonates with me. Intuitively, I feel that my experience of dance was consistent with the principles of yoga. I feel compelled to explore how the form and practice of *Bharatha Natyam* relates to the principles of yoga.

Reviewing the text of *Yogasutra* and its commentaries, I realize the responsibility of accurately presenting multiple interpretations of *ashta anga* by the various translators. While quoting, I plan to use the words of a particular author that best represents the composite understanding and also indicate my resonance with it. The intention is not to suggest that the quoted author is the authority or seminal contributor, but simply one who has chosen the best words to convey an understanding that is shared by other writers on the topic, and one that has emerged from my engagement with the texts and resonates with me.

Yoga - Practice and Outcome

The word *yoga* has come to represent physical practices, and is "largely divorced from its historical and spiritual roots" (Whicher & Carpenter, 2003, p. 1). The root word *yuj* suggests yoking together to join (Feuerstein, 2003). Looking at it from this perspective, yoga is interpreted as practices that facilitate union of "mind power with cosmic power" (Yogananda, 1997, p. 322). However, if we consider that the root word is *yuja* (sense of concentration) and not *yuji* (conjunction), then yoga is a practice of concentration (Feuerstein, 1998, p. 8). It is then suggestive of a conjunction that comes about, through a practice of concentration.

Yoga also means *samadhi* (per Panini's grammarian text) which Digambarji interprets as "yoga is a way to go to *samadhi*" (1975, p. 29). Feuerstein concurs that yoga is *Samadhi* and includes both the "techniques of unifying consciousness and the resulting state of ecstatic union with the object of contemplation" (1998, pp. 3–4). Yoga, then is a practice of focused concentration that leads to the outcome of *samadhi*. Vyasa describes this process of *samadhi* as "placing - putting together" (Feuerstein, 1998, p. 3). In this sense, yoga is both the outcome of *samadhi* and the practices that lead up to *samadhi*.

The practice of concentrated focus carves a path towards *samadhi*—a path that is the experience of meditative immersion. Swami Rama writes that while concentration is to narrow down and focus—it leads to an expansive state that is meditation (1986, p. 12). With sustained concentration, this meditative experience then leads to the next state wherein the *Yogi* forgets self—identity. Chaudhuri wrote that this is when the "focus on meditation" acts as a "path to *Samadhi*" (1965, p. 118). *Samadhi* is the name given to what must be "passed through" to attain "freedom" and liberation (*kaivalya*) which is the "object of yoga" (Shrivastava, 1987, p. 47). This process of yoga that teaches the process of "dis-identification" from the phenomenal world is described in *Yogasutra* (Whicher, 1998).

At this level of understanding, yoga is the praxis that facilitates communion between self and the cosmic self, through concentration and expansive meditation that can ultimately lead to liberation and self-transcendence.

Yogasutra

The *Yogasutra,* attributed to sage Patanjali is the first known separate treatise on yoga and has a special place in the history of yoga (Shastri, 1975, pp. 15–17). It is the earliest known systematic statement of philosophical insights and practical psychology that define yoga (Miller, 1995, p. 1). While the *Yogasutra* is "neither sacred scripture nor historical artifact," it presents a "set of philosophical analyses that probe timeless dilemmas of cognition and obstacles to spiritual tranquility" (Miller, 1995, p. ix). Feuerstein recommends the *Yogasutra* as the "best entry point into the theoretical side of yoga" (Bharati, 2001, p. xv).

The *Yogasutra* is written in Sanskrit using the simple writing style of *sutra* and has about 195 aphorisms that are divided into four parts—*Samadhi pada, sadhana pada, vibhuti pada,* and *kaivalya pada* (Shrivastava, 1987, p. 14). The second and third *pada* describe eight limbs (*ashta anga*) of Yogic practice that lead to "cessation of thought and cultivation of pure contemplation" (Miller, 1995, p. 18).

Patanjali described the criterion of yoga as cessation of fluctuations of mind (*chitta vritti nirodha*) with a sense of detachment and dis-identification (*vairagya*) that is inherent in complete surrender to the Universal force (*Ishvara pranidhana*) (Shastri, 1975, p. 17). While Miller described thought as *chitta* (1995, p. xii), Digambarji suggests that *chitta* is the entity responsible for all "fluctuations in mind" (1975, p. 29).

The *Rig Veda* dated around 3000 BCE describes yoga in the sense of 'effecting a connection' and other later literature from 500–600 BCE. use the concept as a way "of controlling senses" (Shrivastava, 1987, pp. 8–9). The *Upanishads* describe the various limbs (such as *asana*, *pranayama*, etc.) and the literature of Manu, Yagnavalkya and others describe some of the Yogic practices (Shastri, 1975, p. 15). With the writing of *Yogasutra*, Patanjali came to be known as the "father of yoga" (Satchidananda, 1990, p. xii). Some commentators identify Hiranyagarbha as the original expounder of yoga, as referenced in *Ahirbudhnya Samhita* (Shastri, 1975, p. 15). However, Feuerstein suggests that Hiranyagarbha is a reference to the primal cosmic force or golden womb from which yoga was born and not to the author of *Yogasutra* (1998, p. 285). He clarifies that yoga may have been a revelation to *Yogi* while in an altered state of awareness (1998, p. 285).

Feuerstein wrote that the *Yogasutra* was probably compiled between 100 BCE and 500 CE (1998, p. 85) and the name Patanjali was the family name of Vedic priest Asurayana, and does not refer to Patanjali, the author of the commentary, *Mahabashya* on Panini's grammar text (1998, p. 284). Mukherji cited the *Brhadaranyaka Upanishad* in concurring that Patanjali was a family name and not unique to one person (1981, p. xi). Miller wrote that the *Yogasutra* is dated around the third century CE based on writing style, concepts, and speculated time of its author (1995, p. 6). Narayanan suggested that "among the six philosophies" in India, Yoga is considered the fifth, placing the *Yogasutra* around the second century CE (2011,p. 4). Mukherji however stated that dating of the *Yogasutra* is inconclusive (1981, pp. xi–xiii).

Yardi (1979, pp. 3–4) speculated on more than one author writing the fourth part of *Yogasutra* while Bharati (2001) and Feuerstein (1998, p. 285) considered Patanjali to be the single mind that compiled and systematized the text. However, Feuerstein also states with certainty that he considers Patanjali's writings to expound the philosophy of *kriya yoga* and the *sutra* describing *ashta-anga* "appear to be quoted" and not the original writings of Patanjali (1989, p. 59). He suggested that Patanjali has been credited with its authorship while he may have incorporated an existing set of aphorisms into his work on *kriya yoga*.

The earliest commentary on the *Yogasutra*, commonly referred to as *Yoga Bhashya* was written by Vyasa and is dated around fifth century CE of Buddhist philosophy and terms such as *niroda* suggest that Vyasa's commentary was written probably around eighth century CE (Miller, 1995, p. 6). Feuerstein described that the word *vyasa* refers to 'collector' (or collator) and can be misleading in suggesting that it referred to just one person by that name (1998, p. 311). Ashok Aklujkar's work on the identity of this Vyasa amongst 28 other writers also named Vyasa, led to his suggestion that it was Vindhya Vyasa who wrote the Yoga Bhashya (Bharati, 2001). Yardi offered further clarification that this was not Veda Vyasa as Vacaspati and Vijnana Bhiksu suggested; nor was it Badarayana Vyasa who wrote the Brahmasutra; but this commentator Vyasa, was another writer who was familiar with language of Buddhist philosophy and theory (1979, pp. 5–6). Janacek's work in 1958 investigating the identity of the author of *Yogasutra* and Mahabashya provides further corroboration that multiple writers by the same name may have lived within a span of a few hundred years (Bharati, 2001).

After about sixteenth century CE *Hata Yoga* and *Raja Yoga* became two distinct practices besides *kriya yoga, jnana yoga, mantra yoga,* and others (Shastri, 1975, p. 18). In Hata yoga practice, Adinatha originated *Nathasampradayic* literature that later described concepts such as *nadi, sushumna, kundalini shakti, etc.* (Shastri, 1975, p. 20). Matsyendranath, his disciple taught Gorakshanatha, whose numerous disciples wrote later *Hata* Yoga texts such as *Gorakshasataka, Hatapradipika,* and *Gheranda Samhita* (Shastri, 1975, p. 18).

"Yoga is union with supreme Universal spirit" and *Raja Yoga* is "king of yoga" (Sivananda, 1960, p. 3). *Raja Yoga* (royal yoga) was masterfully systematized by Patanjali in *Yogasutra* (Yogananda, 1997, p. 266). In 1893, at the World Parliament of Religions in Chicago, Vivekananda spoke on the essence of *Raja Yoga* based on the *Yogasutra* as understood by his mentor, Ramakrishna Paramahamsa (Miller, 1995, p. xi). He expounded that the purpose of *Raja Yoga* is to teach the nature of Self and Universe (Shrivastava, 1987, p. 3). The *Yogasutra* describes eight (*ashta*) limbs (*anga*) as guiding principles that lead to intuitive knowing and integration of body and mind; seen and seer; matter and energy; *prakriti* and *purusha* (Iyengar, 2008, p. 130).

Ashta Anga

Patanjali states that the guiding principles of *ashta anga* provide a sevenfold path for intuitive knowledge (*prajnya*) (Satchidananda, 1990, p. 119). The eight constituent practices or *ashta anga* are *yama* (moral principles), *niyama* (observances), *asana* (posture), *pranayama* (breath control), *pratyahara* (withdrawal of senses), *dharana* (concentration), *dhyana* (meditation) and *samadhi* (pure contemplation) (Miller, 1995, p. 52). While the practices of *ashta anga yoga* are critical in defining a practice as yoga, discipline, regularity of practice, and developing a dispassionate Yogic outlook are also important criteria for a Yogic practice (Narayanan, 2012).

While each school of yoga practices these principles uniquely different from the other, there seems to be concurrence in their desired outcome. This is represented by Feuerstein in the 'Wheel of Yoga' wherein each spoke in the wheel leads to the center—the outer rim representing *yama* and *niyama*, the central hub wheel marked as *Samadhi* with its core of self-transcendence (1998, p. 35). The spokes of the wheel are described as practices of selfless service as in *karma yoga*, devotional love of *bhakti yoga*, yoga of action in *kriya yoga*, path of knowledge or *jnana yoga*, *hata yoga*, *mantra yoga* and so on.

Wheel of Yoga

This representation of yoga presents an unified symbol that incorporates at least three *anga* from the eight described in *Yogasutra*. *Yama* and *niyama* are suggested to be the outer structure and underpinnings that are essential for any practice of yoga. *Samadhi* as a process leading to transcendence of self is depicted as the center hub in all practices of yoga. Each school of yoga builds on *yama* and *niyama* principles and works towards the central goal of *samadhi* leading to the core of self-transcendence.

The literature review for this study has also suggested a similar understanding. Iyengar who developed his own school of *hata yoga* practices, writes that "in yoga . . . many may take one path as a key in order to experience self-realization . . . but I say that there is absolutely no difference between the various practices of yoga" (1995).

Prominent Yogi and teacher of Integral Yoga, Swami Satchidananda even suggests discretion in practicing *ashta anga*. In a discourse titled "Transcending Body and mind"(Satchidananda Ashram-Yogaville, 2002), he states that there is no need to follow specific practices of *asana* if one is able to enter a meditative state without any physical postures.

Bharati refers to Vyasa's commentary when he writes that "*Samadhi* for qualified some may be achieved without aid of any *anga*" (2001, pp. 7–8) and cites the historical stories of Sishupala and Jada Bharatha who relied only on the practice of the internal limbs of *dharana*, and *dhyana* to reach *samadhi* (the practice of these three anga as a continuum is referred to as *samyama)* (Mukherji, 1981, p. 253). This branch of *dhyana yoga* emphasizes meditative immersion (Shastri, 1975, p. 15).

The first four principles of *yama*, *niyama*, *asana* and *pranayama* are categorized as working on external physical aspects of the mind/body (*bahiranga sadhana)* while *pratyahara* leading to *samyama*, work on the inner nonphysical aspects of mind—body(*antaranga sadhana*) (Iyengar, 2008, p. 167). Bharati voices a shared understanding that *kriya yoga* is a good practice of the external limbs, where "practice itself is yoga" (2001, p. 8). This view is supported by Krishnamacharya in describing *kriya yoga* as the yoga of action that "includes fiery aspiration, learning of the scriptures and total surrender to Lord consciousness" (1976, p. 21). In contrast, *Raja Yoga* also focuses on enhancing the ability and intensity of concentration (Sivananda, 1970, p. ix).

Yama

The *Yogasutra* describes *yama* as five observances (restraint)—*ahimsa*, *satya*, *asteya*, *brahmacharya*, *and aparigraha*. These are stated to be universal human values that transcend temporal and spatial boundaries. *Ahimsa* is interpreted as the moral principle of not causing injury, *satya* as truthfulness and *asteya* as not stealing (Digambarji, Jha, & Sahay 1984, p. 6).

Brahmacharya is commonly understood as a practice of celibacy that "transforms energy of procreation into spiritual energy" (Iyengar, 2008, p. 143). Satchidananda explains that when *Brahmacharya* is "established, vigor is gained" (1990, p. 137). Sivananda clarifies that "repression of sexual energy is not brahmacharya—it is freedom from urge" (1960, p. 35). Feuerstein elaborates that *brahmacharya* is "one who is brahmic"—whose behavior "imitates the condition of the Absolute (*Brahman*) which is asexual" (1998, pp. 12–13). The word *brahmacharya* literally means "walk(ing) in *Brahman*" as if moving in constant congruence with Brahman (Rama, 1983).

Reviewing the multiple understandings of *brahmacharya*, it seems like each speaks to a specific aspect of this larger principle. If the essence is to continually seek the Absolute, practices that are conducive to this quest may be considered consistent with the concept of *brahmacharya*. In contrast, restraining oneself from practices that distract and detract from this quest may also be considered *brahmacharya*. Simply said, the observance of *brahmacharya* may include physical and mental discipline including restraint. Swami Sivananda summarizes this best, where he states that *brahmacharya* refers to the mental and physical observances through which the Yogi can "attain/reach Brahman" (1970, p. 24). He states that the mind is "purified" by following the principle of *yama* and "as you think, so you become" (1960, pp. 17–18).

Aparigraha is described as "not coveting" or "not seeking to possess," but Vasishta replaces this principle in his commentary (Digambarji, 1984, p. 6). He adds six other concepts to the list of *yama* such as forgiveness, compassion, and straightforwardness. For the purpose of this study, I propose to adhere to the five *yama* described in *Yogasutra*.

Niyama

Yama along with *niyama* form the foundation of yoga (Sivananda, 1970, p. 83). They are ethical preparation for any practice of yoga (Shrivastava, 1987, p. 42). *Niyama* are described as five disciplined practices of *saucha*, *santosha*, *tapas*, *svadhyaya*, and *Ishvara pranidhana*. There is consensus amongst commentators that *saucha* refers to cleanliness, *santosha* to contentment, *tapas* to religious fervor, *svadhyaya* to study of self and scriptures, and *Isvara Pranidhana* to complete surrender to the Ultimate force (also called God). However, Feuerstein is vehement in stating that *Isvara* is not Lord, or an Absolute but simply a "special self in contrast to the human transcending self"— *isvara* refers to a Self that has never foregone Self-awareness; a Self that has never been limited by finite consciousness; a Self that has never been involved in the mechanism of *prakriti* (1989, p. 16).

In *hata yoga* and *laya yoga* the emphasis on cleanliness is an extensive practice of *shat karma*—cleansing of various systems in the body such as digestive, olfactory, musculature, breathing, etc. (Muktibodhananda, 2000, p. 186). Other commentators interpret *tapas* as religious fervor—this may well be one aspect of self-study that accomplishes the larger goal of establishing internal purity. *Svadhyaya* includes study of scriptures, self-inquiry and suggests an attitude of curiosity to learn, in service of self-improvement towards the ultimate goal of knowing the Absolute (Satchidananda, 1990, p. 149).

In many ways, *yama* and *niyama* appear to be two aspects of the same. In one's quest for the Absolute, embracing the principles of *yama* and practicing *niyama* define the attitude of the *Yogi* as one who is introspective, inquisitive, disciplined, discriminating, and aspiring to be reflective of the Absolute at each given moment in time.

What adds energy to this attitude is *Ishvara pranidhana*—an approach of total surrender to the Ultimate, referred to as *Ishvara*. Inherent in this devotion and dedication to *Ishvara*, are elements such as acceptance without egoistic assessment. This ability to transcend self cultivates the attitude of a dispassionate observer—one who is able to fully experience life without judging any part of the experience. It also fosters the development of a cosmic identity with loving acceptance of guidance by a higher entity symbolized as *Ishvara*.

Sivananda described *Ishvara Pranidhana* as a form of *bhakti yoga*—a practice of devotional love, which softens the heart while loving for love's sake (1970, p. 91). However, Diwakar considers self-surrender to be inclusive of several faculties or power, unlike *bhakti yoga* that builds on the single emotion of love (1975, p. 7). Sivananda reiterates that *jnana* (knowledge) is the fruit of *bhakti yoga* and "perfect knowledge is love" (1970, p. x). Feuerstein cites the *Bhakti-sutra* of Narada from 1000 CE that places *bhakti* above all other paths describing it as the "quintessence of love immortality"—a love that is "devoid of qualities" (1998, pp. 55–59).

The *Yogasutra* describes *yama* and *niyama* in about fifteen descriptive *sutra* before finally stating that through surrender to God, *samadhi* is achieved. The essence of surrender to the Ultimate as reflected in everyday choices and interactions appear to be a prerequisite for any yoga practice. The image of Feuerstein's wheel with the outer rim of *yama* and *niyama* is consistent with the composite understanding that observance of these human values is a lifelong Yogic practice. With each turn of the wheel, through a process of self-introspection and discrimination, one strives to act consistent with the workings of the larger cosmic order.

Asana

The *Yogasutra* dedicates three *sutra* of about a dozen words to *asana*. It describes *asana* as "any steady and comfortable posture" (Sivananda, 1970, p. 97). Satchidananda concurs by stating that any comfortable posture that is conducive to meditation qualifies as *asana* (1990, p. 152). *Asana* is also described as an effortless state of complete absorption (*samapati*) in the posture—Iyengar described it as "repose in the pose" (2008, p. 149). The practice of *asana* is to end "duality" between body and mind, mind and soul (Iyengar, 2008, p. 151). Another example cited is that of pain and pleasure—a pair of opposites that are experienced with the "senses contact objects of the world" and yoga is freedom from this type of experience of opposites (Ajaya, 1980, p. 361).

The *Yogasutra* does not describe a specific practice or posture for *asana*. There is no mention of bodily postures in texts of *Samhita* (Shastri, 1975, p. 13). Singleton questions if *asana* as physical postures were a later non-Indian practice (2010). However, Vyasa has described several postures while interpreting the term *asana*. Feuerstein writes that *asana* was simply a meditational aid for Patanjali, without specified postural practices (1989, p. 90). Swami Rama suggests that the physical aspect of *asana* practice is to facilitate the ability for meditation while seated with back straight and neck aligned with spine (1983, pp. 130–131).

The original nature of *asana* as a steady and comfortable sitting posture helpful for meditative practices became relegated into the background, and *asana* became a particular posture of the body (Shastri, 1975, p. 14). The word *asana* means the seat on which Yogic practices are performed (Diwakar, 1975, p. 13). Etymology of '*as*' in *asana* is "to sit" and can refer to where one sits, how one sits, and how one gets to the sitting state (Bharati, 2001, p. 568). The common factor amongst all *asana* is keeping the "head, neck and trunk straight and balanced" (Bharati, 2001, p. 570). Mukherji concurs that in all *asana*, the spine has to be kept straight, holding the body steady with a focused mind (1981, p. 228).

The interpretation of *asana* as practice of physical postures is seen in the school *of hata yoga* and *laya* yoga, where its practice "opens up energy channels and psychic centers" within the body (Muktibodhananda, 2000, p. 67). In *Raja Yoga*, the suggestion is that *asana* as a physical practice serves to lessen the "natural tendency for restlessness" thereby facilitating meditation on the infinite (Satchidananda, 1990, p. 154).

Reviewing interpretations of several commentators, it is fair to surmise that *asana* presents the *anga* that works on the physical aspect of the body. It refers to the use of the body in a way that is steady, balanced and with ease. Steady is not necessarily stationary—it is not only a static pose—it can be a use of the body wherein there is consistent stability and ease. As pointed out by some authors, the common element in *asana* that seems to coincide with steadiness is holding the spine straight. Keeping the head, neck and back aligned does not exclude an inclined posture or even lying down on the floor.

Even while practicing postural *asana,* there is movement that is necessary to get into and out of a pose. The suggestion is to ease into and out of poses, all the while being attuned to the experience of the posture and/or movement, so that there is complete absorption in the *asana.* For the purpose of this study, I would consider a modified interpretation and describe *asana* as moving the body with ease, ensuring stability, and being engrossed in the process.

Pranayama

In just five *sutra,* the concept of *pranayama* is described as discretely interrupted flow of inhaled and exhaled breath—regulating the flow of breath. Some interpret breath as *prana* or life force, the essence of all energy that is manifested as breath (Ramacharaka, 1969, p. 19). And when the energy flow of *prana* is enhanced, it is a practice of *pranayama* (Muktibodhananda, 2000, p. 149).

Bharati interprets *pranayama* as stabilizing of *prana* flow in the entire body (2001, p. 623). While the *Yogasutra* does not describe any specific breathing exercise to regulate the flow, it does describe that the pause between exhalation and inhalation is long and subtle. *Pranayama* is the creation of these phases of suspended breath (Mukherji, 1981, p. 235). Besides exhaled, inhaled and suspended breath there is a fourth type of breath that transcends the others (Miller, 1995, p. 58). It operates beyond external and internal realms (Bharati, 2001, p. 619).

It is a fourth level of *pranayama* where there is no concentration on retention—it is automatic (Satchidananda, 1990, p. 161). Feuerstein suggests this state of *pranayama* is a physiological "correlate of an extraordinary state of consciousness" being experienced by the Yogi. At the fourth level, the regulation of *prana* that is not deliberate is referred to as *nirbija pranayama* (Iyengar, 2008, p. 152).

The role of *pranayama* is to settle the body and prepare the mind for concentration. Iyengar believes in following the linear pattern suggested by Patanjali in that *pranayama* should be practiced only after perfection of postural *asana* (Iyengar, 2008, p. 152). However, while deliberate breathing exercise can be practiced with discretion, automatic and spontaneous breathing is an ongoing, co-occurring *anga*. While *asana* and *pranayama* are described separately as two *anga*, breath clearly is integrated within the practice of any *asana*, unless deliberately suspended for a certain period of time.

One type of breathing practice is to regulate the duration of inhalation, another is to regulate exhalation, and a third to regulate the time and space between the two. The fourth of non-deliberate breathing is suggestive of breath that is consistent with physical and/or mental activity that is practiced while leading towards a state of meditative engrossment.

Pratyahara

Patanjali described in two *sutra* that *pratyahara* is when the attention is turned inward, by withdrawing sensory stimulation of the mind—when the mind is controlled, sense organs are drawn inward by the mind (Sivananda, 1960, p. 56). Vyasa describes this metaphorically— "when a queen bee flies up, all the bees swarm after her; when she settles down—they settle" (Feuerstein, 1989, p. 94). Similarly, when the external sensory stimulation ceases, the conscious mind quiets down and is drawn inwards. *Pratyahara* is an internal engagement of the senses—suggesting a transcendence of the natural world (Chaudhuri, 1965, p. 55). When the senses are withdrawn from the phenomenal world, "they can be yoked to serve the soul" (Iyengar, 2008, p. 159). And, through *pratyahara* the ultimate control of the senses is achieved (Bharati, 2001, p. 645).

Pratyahara suggests a responsive and stimulated engagement with internal stimulus—it is withdrawing the sensory stimulation from the external towards an internal engagement. It suggests preoccupation of the eyes and ears, by their focus on an internal stimulus. It implies a mind that is inattentive to what is seen and heard externally—a mind that is instead concentrated on an inner experience.

Pratyahara has the element of inner focus or concentration as its prerequisite. It is the focus on the inner stimulus that facilitates the *anga* of *pratyahara*. Shastri suggests that *pratyahara* along with concentration (*dharana*) is a preliminary state of meditation (*dhyana*) (1975, p. 15). It acts similar to an entrance foyer that leads to the doorway of concentration (*dharana*)—a doorway that is initially restrictive before opening into an expansive meditative space (*dhyana*).

Dharana

Yogasutra describes in one sutra that *dharana* (single pointed focus) is the fixation of *chitta* (understood as mind, awareness, consciousness, thought, etc.) on a particular point in space (Mukherji, 1981, p. 249). "When thoughts are deeply concentrated in the region where the mind is focused, it is *dharana*" (Kripalvananda, 1977). Sivananda described "absolute one-pointed-ness" of the mind as the cause and outcome of complete control of senses (1960, p. 57). Chaudhuri suggests that *dharana* is maintaining focus on the meditative path leading to *samadhi* (1965, p. 118). Satchidananda described *dharana* as focusing on an object (1990, p. 171), while Iyengar described *dharana* as controlling thoughts and disturbances (in the mind) (Iyengar, 2008, p. 169). Initially holding focus on objects is easier than focus on "objects of senses" as the resulting engagement is delayed and harder in the latter (Mukherji, 1981, p. xviii).

The ability to concentrate is a "necessary condition for yoga" and Yogic concentration is described as holding the "same thought constant for some time" (Mukherji, 1981, p. xvii). Swami Sivananda suggests a time duration for practice of concentration— he described *dharana* as holding focus for 12 seconds; *dhyana* for 12 x 12 seconds; and *samadhi* for 12 x 12 x 12 seconds (1960, p. 61).

This practice of one-pointed concentration appears to be a critical *anga* that serves to accomplish the previous *anga* of *pratyahara*. Just as *pranayama* is a necessary *anga* for the practice of *asana* so too, *dharana* is essential to the practice of *pratyahara*. Said differently, *dharana* facilitates proper practice of *asana*, *pranayama* and *pratyahara* and is itself an outcome of their proper practice. *Dharana* is both a prerequisite and an outcome—and, yoga is predicated on concentration and is also a practice of concentration.

Dhyana - Samadhi

When in this state of intense concentration (*dharana*), there emerges an interactive engagement between the Yogi and the object focused upon. When the thoughts begin to flow continuously towards the focus of *dharana*, the next meditative state of *dhyana* emerges (Kripalvananda, 1977). Swami Rama is quoted as saying that "meditation is expansion" and not possible without concentration (Ballentine, 1986, p. 12). In this meditative state, a sense of oneness emerges. The distinction between the Yogi and the object of focus becomes diffuse. The meditative engagement between the experiencer and experienced is *dhyana*, the intensity of which can be complete immersion and engrossment in the meditative process. When meditating in this state of "forgetting oneself" the next stage *samadhi* emerges (Mukherji, 1981, p. 252).

Dhyana culminates in *samadhi* (Shastri, 1975, p. 15). When "one's own consciousness does not intervene, *dhyana* flows into *samadhi*" (Iyengar, 2008, p. 170). In *samadhi*, the "experiencer and experienced" become one (Sivananda, 1970, p. 303). When there is single-pointed concentration on an object it is *dharana*; when there is a "continuous flow of cognition towards object"—it is *dhyana*; and in that meditative state, when there is no separation between the two (devoid of form)—it is *samadhi* (Satchidananda, 1990, pp. 171–173). When "form dissolves" in meditation, it is *samadhi* (Kripalvananda, 1977).

Samadhi has been described as an experiential state of "spiritual rapture" that goes beyond "senses and perceptions" (Sadhu, 1962, p. 16). However, Feuerstein clarifies that *Samadhi* is not external to self or ecstasy, but really an inner experience of "entasy" (Feuerstein, 1998, p. 4). When the meditative absorption becomes so deep, that the mind which is fixed on the object forgets its own self, such voluntary concentration is *samadhi*; meditation forgetting oneself is *samadhi* (Mukherji, 1981, p. 12). In the state of oneness (*dhyana*), "as if completely voiding the form" the experience of that inner understanding is *samadhi*.

When the *anga* of *dharana – dhyana - samadhi* are practiced as a continuum, their conjoint process is *samyama* which leads to intuitive knowledge or *prajnya* that transcends temporal constraints of past and future (Mukherji, 1981, p. 253). By focusing *samyama* on a specific object, *prajnya* of a specified nature results - for example, *samyama* on the Sun leads to *prajnya* of the world (Feuerstein, 1989, p. 109). At its most intense, this experience of "spiritual union" in *samadhi* eventually replaces perception with "pure awareness, independent of objective duality" (De Marquette, 1965, p. 197). At this state of *samadhi,* according to Patanjali, the *prajnya* or realization of the transcendental Self amounts to "genuine everlasting freedom" that goes beyond phenomenal dimensions (Feuerstein, 1998, p. 342). Kripalvananda described the fruits of *samadhi* as purity of spirit, *rtambara prajnya* (highest wisdom), divine body, miraculous powers (*siddhi*), and liberation (1977, p. 1). *Rtambara prajnya* or highest wisdom is gained while in this state of *samadhi* (Mukherji, 1981, p. 105).

Prajnya of any magnitude suggests the presence of an active mind where there is an implied separation between subject and object. *Prajnya* suggests the presence of an entity that observes, experiences and obtains intuitive knowledge. While *samadhi* may be a state wherein this knowledge becomes accessible, a subject/object distinction is essential for receiving (and recognizing) of this wisdom (Kripalvananda, 1977, p. 40). It is only when the mind re-emerges that the experience of *prajnya* is possible (Sadhu, 1962, p. 45). The state of *samadhi* which allows for *prajnya* is called *samprajnya samadhi*.

Samprajnyata samadhi has consciousness of the object (Whicher, 1997, p. 2); wherein there is a presence of thought or reasoning. It occurs through the "accompaniment of the appearances of gross thought (*vitarka*), subtle thought (*vicara*), ecstasy (*ananda*) and I-am-ness (*asmita)*" (Arya, 1986, p. 218). Stated differently, there can be four states of meditative engrossment (*samapati*) en route to *samprajnyata samadhi* viz. *savitarka, savicara, sananda,* and *sasmita* (Kripalvananda, 1977, p. 3). At each level, when there is transcendence of thought, reflection, bliss and I-am-ness, the stepping stone to the next level is correspondingly termed *nirvitarka, nirvicara, nirananda, nirasmita* each paving the way to the next level up towards a state of *samprajnyata samadhi* (Feuerstein, 1998, p. 335). Kriyananda proposed that these are really nine stages of *samadhi* and are *savitarka, nirvitarka, vicara, nirvicara, ananda, asmita, purusha khyati* (knowing self and other), *asamprajnyata samadhi, and dharma megha samadhi* (1985, pp. 320–323). C. R. Narayanan (personal communication, February 8, 2012) suggested that the attributes of *savicara, nirvicara, ananda,* and *asmita* may be attributes of a reflective Yogic attitude that may not necessarily be a descriptor of *samapati*. The various descriptive stages or attributes of *samapati* are considered the experience of initial stages of *samadhi* as the Yogi moves further along this continuum from *dhyana* (immersion).

If *samprajnya samadhi* is one-pointed engrossment, in contrast, *asamprajnyata samadhi* is a state where even the engrossment dissolves (Mukherji, 1981, p. xix). In *samprajnya* state the mind is conscious of the object of focus, whereas in *asamprajnya* there is a higher level of super-consciousness where there is no awareness of the object of focus (Shrivastava, 1987, p. 49). While *asamprajnya* is commonly described as a higher state of *samadhi* that transcends *samprajnya samadhi*, it is to be noted that Patanjali does not use the word *asamprajnya* (Sahai, 1975, pp. 25–26).

When *samadhi* is assisted by focus on object, it is also referred to as *sabija samadhi* (Mukherji, 1981, p. xviii). The higher level of complete absorption that is not assisted by focus on object is called *nirbija samadhi* (Kripalvananda, 1977). Shrivastava suggests that there is no *prajnya* at this level of *samadhi* (1987, p. 25). However, Yogi have described their brief experiences at this stage as "not *samapati or samadhi*"—it has been called "sunya" with no words to express it (Sahai, 1975, pp. 25–26). Inability to express an experience does not nullify the experience or suggest that there is no *prajnya* that emerges in this state. In the context of this study, this aspect is not explored further.

Samadhi is both a "state and process" wherein the finite being loses self in the "sea of cosmic *samadh*i (tranquility)" (Chakravarthi, 1974, p. 95). If *samadhi* is a process, the manifestation of this process is the experience of ecstasy (Sadhu, 1962, p. 45). Nelson writes that knowing is "both the act of immediate experiencing as well as the experience of that experiencing" (2000, p. 55). Yogi who stay alive, describe experiencing a temporary state of *samadhi* called *kevala samadhi* where the mind that is fully immersed, reverts back into 'normal' state of consciousness even while holding on to an experience of "immense bliss" (Sadhu, 1962, pp. 171–173).

When the mind is dissolved completely and irreversibly, the *Yogi* is in *sahaja samadhi* which is perennial and accompanied by release from incarnations (Sadhu, 1962, p. 171). Sankaracharya in his *Viveka Choodamani* stated that "salvation is possible only with knowledge of union with the spirit" (Sadhu, 1962, p. 13). When the human mind goes beyond speech and merges with cosmic mind it is *samadhi* (Chakravarti, 1974). *Samadhi* is the ultimate negation of everything relative and temporal (Sadhu, 1962, p. 153). At this state of self-transcendence that emerges from *dharma megha samadhi* the self is liberated from life—it transcends the phenomenal natural world—this liberation, *kaivalya*, is the goal of yoga.

The concept of *samadhi* suggests a wide range of experiencing oneness that emerges in evolved states of immersion (*samapati*) and continues up to and beyond *dharma megha samadhi*. At its preliminary stages, the experience of *samadhi* is considered to be *samapati*. As the intensity and depth of oneness increases in *samadhi*, *prajnya* emerges. When a Yogi develops the ability to transcend space and time, the possibility of *dharma megha samadhi* emerges, leading to liberation or *kaivalya*. In the context of this study, the aim is to discuss *natya* as a practice of *yoga* that paves the way towards *dhyana* and *samadhi*, even if only to a preliminary stage comparable to *samapati*.

In this regard, the *anga* of *asana*, *pratyahara*, *dharana* and *dhyana* are especially relevant to this study. The external and physical form of *asana* leads to the internal experience of *dhyana*, through the focus developed in *dharana* as evidenced by *pratyahara*. The correlation between *rasa* and the meditative immersion in *dhyana* leading to *samadhi* is an integral part of this study. The discussion on the form of *Bharatha Natyam* as an embodiment of *ashta anga yoga* is taken up in Chapter 7, while Chapter 8 explores the correlation between *rasa*, the experience of *Bharatha Natyam* and meditative immersion, the experience of yoga.

7. DANCING IN THE MIDDLE: FORM OF BHARATHA NATYAM

Bharatha Natyam as an Embodied Practice of Ashta Anga

I started this study on *Bharatha Natyam* with a quest to understand my experience of dancing. How does this experience change with audience presence and engaged participation? Can the experience exist even while the dancer was consciously unaware of it? And, what is my dancing experience called? I had associated the word *rasa* with the experience of dancing. And I wanted to how *rasa* was described in the text of *Natyasastra*. What is its role in *natya*? My parallel process is to understand how the explanations from *Natyasastra* apply to *Bharatha Natyam* as a stylized form and expressive experience.

The *Natyasastra* unequivocally states that the purpose of *natya* is to evoke *rasa*. Descriptions on melody, rhythm, ideal musical instruments and role of singer/dancer are from the perspective of how each aspect contributes towards evoking *rasa* in the audience. The role of the actor/dancer is to step into the role of the character being depicted and convey the emotional experience of the character to the audience—once again, to evoke *rasa* in the viewer/listener. While answering some existing questions, my engagement with *Natyasastra* created new questions.

If *rasa* describes audience experience, what describes a dancer's experience? If movement (*nritta*) has no interpretive purpose, yet is an integral part of *natya* that evokes *rasa*—then, what is the relevance of *nritta* in creating *rasa*? If *rasa* experience (*rasa vada*) is twin to a mystical experience (*brahmasvada*)—was there a different conceptual framework that explains the dancing experience? There are at least two distinct aspects of my study— the form (*nritta*) of *Bharatha Natyam*, and the experience of dancing (*rasa*). I am suggesting that the vocabulary of *ashta anga* provides a language to link the dancing form (*nritta*) and its experience (*rasa*).

How Does Bharatha Natyam Embody the Form of Ashta Anga Yoga?

Yogasutra describes the context of *ashta anga* in practice of yoga towards a goal of *samadhi*, leading to self-transcendence and liberation (*kaivalya*). There are at least two physical *anga* that give form to a practice of yoga—*asana* and *pranayama*. Along with physical discipline and mental outlook, these *anga* pave the way to a meditative immersion in *dhyana* leading to *samadhi*. I propose to discuss the aspects of form and experience of *Bharatha Natyam* as they correspond to specific *anga*.

The practice of *ashta anga yoga* leading to the experience of *samadhi* hinges on a Yogi's ability to concentrate. Without concentration (*dharana*) any practice of yoga may be self-limiting in the intensity of its experience. I understand *dharana* to evidence the readiness of a *Yogi* to engage in meditation (*dhyana*). *Dharana* acts as a doorway that can be entered through only when there are no significant distractions (physical or mental). In order to prepare for entry through this doorway, the suggestion is to align physical and mental aspects through practice of *asana* and *pranayama*. *Asana* is use of the body to balance internal energies. *Prana* is the breath of life—energizing and regulating its flow (calming, steadying or enhancing) is a practice of *pranayama*. While concentration may be possible anytime (even if transient or at lower intensities), the level of concentration required to enter the doorway of *dharana* leading to *dhyana* is when mental and physical distractions are controlled, suggesting a deeper and more intense focus of attention.

When this happens, the state of mind is representative of *pratyahara* wherein the external sensory stimulation is controlled and the attention turns inwards, towards the object (or lack of object) focused upon in *dharana*. At this point, a Yogi becomes ready to engage in meditation. As the intensity of concentration increases, an expansive meditative state emerges. In this expansive state, an interaction can emerge between the active (participant) self and the object of concentration (or lack of object). This nonverbal dialogue or communication between the two entities (self and another) may lead to a higher state of *samadhi* where the distinction between the two entities dissolves. It is in this state of *samadhi* (oneness), that an intuitive knowing (*prajnya*) can emerge. However, in order to become aware of this knowing, the active self re-emerges and recognizes the new intuitive knowledge received while in *samadhi*. When a Yogi's physical existence nears its end leading to liberation (*kaivalya*), the Yogi moves beyond *samadhi* to transcend his physical self and the natural world, free from physical existence.

The practice of *ashta anga* towards oneness (*samadhi*) is predicated on concentration. It facilitates a calming of body and mind, shifting the sensory attention and focusing it on the concentrated entity. At this point, the Yogi's ability to sustain and intensify concentration may be dependent on a variety of individual and external factors. The meditative engagement and the Yogi's navigation towards *samadhi* varies in response to personality of the Yogi and also affected by time, space and any distractions experienced by the Yogi. One way to ensure smoother transitions into meditation may be to include *asana* and *pranayama* practices as a prelude to meditation.

The *anga* of *yama* and *niyama* are attitudinal adjustments that help carry over this meditative state beyond the duration of time that one practices yoga. In order to be a successful in the time bound practice of yoga, the mind has to set aside worries and distractions of day to day life. And, in order to be successful beyond the practice time, adhering to *yama* and *niyama* may help reinforce a disciplined and principled life style with a Yogic mind set and outlook.

To describe how the form of *Bharatha Natyam* is a practice of *ashta anga*, I propose to first discuss how this style of dancing practices the values of *yama* and observances of *niyama*. The dancer learns to practice behavior and thinking consistent with these principles, primarily for the purpose of natya. However, with continued practice, it is reasonable to expect that some dancers may very well emulate these dancing practices in their day to day life. When this happens, the dancer becomes a Yogi even after the dancing has stopped. *Yama* and *niyama* are practices that can transform a *natya Yogi* into a lifelong *Yogi*. *Natyam* develops these qualities that can be practiced beyond dance, as a way of Yogic living.

Yama in Bharatha Natyam

Bharatha Natyam is an embodied practice of yoga. It is a practice of *ashta anga* that with repeated practice develops an attitude, outlook and approach to living consistent with *yama* and *niyama*. The ethical principles and observances of *yama* and *niyama* inculcate values of conscientious and harmonic living. These are lifelong practices of repeated self-correction of actions, through honest introspection and perseverance to aspire for a higher level of living as a *Yogi*. While some dancers and *Yogi* may need little effort to live conscientiously, for several it is a process of continuous self-improvement. This is a lifelong aspiration and not necessarily a prerequisite to successful yoga practice.

In this present study, we are not evaluating a dancer as a Yogi - we are exploring how *natya* is yoga. We are inquiring into *Bharatha Natyam* as an embodiment of *ashta anga* principles. As such, *yama* and *niyama* are values for living and apply to the person who is practicing yoga and not to the yoga practice. However, for even an advanced yoga practitioner to become a true Yogi, per the *ashta anga* descriptions, the adherence to *yama* and *niyama* are essential.

Natyasastra describes an ideal dancer as one who "cannot be arrogant, egoistic" and should have "discipline, self-restraint, self-transcendence and humility" (Vatsyayan, 1996, p. 10). For the purpose of this chapter, I am relying on my personal experience of dancing, and teaching *Bharatha Natyam* for several decades. I am approaching this discussion from an assumption that a dancer who is adept at portraying a dance style that retains the integrity of *yama* principles, has internalized much of this embodied practice and is likely to be a person who is embodies the same values in life.

In explaining how *Bharatha Natyam* is an embodiment of a specific *anga*, I speak from my point of view, which may well be shared by several others. It is not my intent to speak on behalf of *Bharatha Natyam* or *Natyasastra*, for that matter. My suggestions are based on my understanding of *Yogasutra,* specifically the *ashta anga* principles and not intended as a scholarly interpretation of *Yogasutra*. While not intended as the last authoritative word on this subject, it is my hope that this will resonate with others and in that sense become generalizable.

Considering the *yama* values of *ahimsa, satya, asteya, brahmacharya* and *aparigraha, Bharatha Natyam* as a dance form is intended to educate and entertain the audience, and the premise is one of non-injury to others. The intent is to bring "peace, entertainment and happiness" and there is no enactment of death in *natya* (Rangacharya, 1986). The principle of *ahimsa* is adhered to in practice of *Bharatha Natyam*—especially emotional injury. In many ways, dancing is intended as a healing salve for emotional pain from discord and conflicts inherent in daily life interactions and events (Rangacharya, 1986).

Authentic representation of a character is essential for an artistic expression and depiction. A dancer's body cannot pretend to know something that it does not know. A dancer cannot dance a movement that the body does not know. A dancer cannot act as if she were experiencing an emotion. Such an inauthentic act by a dancer may look expressive but without the necessary emotional knowing may not convey genuine experience or evoke a corresponding *rasa*. In many ways, as a teacher I often remind my students that the body is slower to learn, and its memory is longer—but the body does not know how to lie. It cannot pretend to move in a way that it does not know how to. The principle of *satya* or truthfulness is embodied in authentic dancing. As stated by Ramakrishna Paramahamsa, if one wishes to "give up false modesty"—dancing and singing is the way (Nikhilananda, 1988, p. 39). While this may refer to dancing as a way to give up false modesty, it also reflects on dancing a practice that encourages authenticity.

Dancing as an active practice does not seek to hold on much less steal another's possession. If the story calls for thievery or the character's personality is that of a thief, the dancer's responsibility is to depict it authentically. But, even in such depictions, in addition to the act of thievery, an accompanying emotional response and loss to another is simultaneously conveyed. The implied message is that stealing causes harm and as a responsible societal member, one should desist from such behaviors. While *natya* shows both the good and bad of the world, the intent is to educate the audience on appropriate and responsible social behavior, such as *asteya* (not stealing).

The dancer strives to be an authentic representation of what the playwright had intended in the lyrics of the poem/song. This attitude of seeking to represent an artistic truism and emulate such a character's behavior may be comparable to Feuerstein's understanding of *brahmacharya* as seeking to emulate *Brahman*

(1998). It is important to bear in mind, that unlike a *Yogi* whose *yama* practices are in his real life, a *Bharatha Natyam* dancer's depiction is while practicing dancing. However, it need not exclude such a dancer from also be a practicing *Yogi* by adhering to *yama* values and observances.

The role assigned to a dancer is one who is authentic, collaborative, working together towards providing the audience an experience—*rasa*. So far, there has been no documentation of what the dancer receives from the action of dancing. While monetary compensations and social popularity are possible - in many ways, dancing is an act of generosity. It is an action of sharing emotions accessed by the dancer, an act of embodied giving. The dancer strives to create an experience for another, holding nothing back for self-enjoyment. It conveys a practice that is designed for complete and total sharing with another. It goes beyond the concept of *aparigraha* in demonstrating generosity without seeking to possess.

These moral observances are natural outcomes from a lifestyle of a disciplined student of dance. The relationship of a *guru - sishya* (teacher - student) tradition builds on the understanding that the student receives several life lessons from the teacher, some of which teach the specific subject such as techniques of dancing. Often, the essential teaching lies in what is not taught - it is learning by observation, emulating a role model, and living by the principles embodied by the teacher. While learning the form and structure of *natya* - the discipline and perseverance that such a practice entails, frequently results in an outcome that embodies a disciplined and principled Yogic outlook.

Niyama in Bharatha Natyam

Niyama are described as five disciplined practices of *saucha, santosha, tapas, svadhyaya,* and *Ishvara pranidhana*. It is reasonable to assume that personal hygiene and cleanliness are habits of human living, and a common expectation. While some schools of yoga practice *shat karma* practice of cleansing self, in *Bharatha Natyam* the relevance of *saucha* is not pronounced. The experience of contentment (*santosha*) and happiness is a *rasa* that is the underpinning of other emotions such as experience of beauty (*sringara*) and laughter (*hasya*). At its most intense the experience of self as its essential Self or *Brahman* has been described as *sat chit ananda* (bliss) (Nikhilananda, 1988, p. 440).

Action that results in "burning of inner impurities" is *tapas* as is its zealous pursuit. The cumulative years of training and practice to become a dancer may also qualify as *tapas*. This combined with *svadhyaya* describes a dancer who is continually learning—about the character, its portrayal, how to convey and relate to a changing body of audience, keeping true to the integrity of the dance, etc. A true dancer is one who is striving to improve, learn, correct and employs all the resources available in order to be authentic and evoke *rasa*. The dancer is in a constant state of responsive attention while performing. What worked for one group of viewers may not for another—the dancer undertakes the responsibility of identifying and responding to the changing needs of an audience. This pursuit of responsive learning and self-teaching could be argued as an illustration of *niyama*.

Isvara Pranidhana is embodied in the dancer, dancing and dance. A dancer who surrenders to be moved; dancing which is the action of surrender and the resulting energy of dance that engages the audience, inspires and evokes *rasa* - when this comes about, the energy in the entire dancing halls becomes electrified. There is a palpable vitality sensed in whatever the dancer is performing - be it rhythmic movement or expressive dancing.

Niyama is an *anga* that is action oriented. *Bharatha Natyam* is a dance that is action oriented. The similarity is in their experience—both that of the practitioner and the viewer. If one were to consider *niyama* a practice of observances that embodied *yama* principles, then *Bharatha Natyam* is an embodiment of both *anga*.

Asana + Pranayama + Dharana →Pratyahara

Nritta represents an integrated practice of the body—it involves the use (*prayoga*) of the feet (legs), hands (arms), eyes (face). *Asana* is understood as a steady, balanced and easy use (*prayoga*) of the body. *Pranayama* is understood as energizing and regulation of breath. *Dharana* is understood as concentration with dedicated (single-pointed) focus. *Pratyahara* is understood as withdrawing senses inwards, from external stimulation. The suggestion of *pratyahara* having a vibrational component is also considered in the following discussion on these *anga* as embodied in the practice of *Bharatha Natyam*.

Prayoga of Eyes

Following the dictates of *Natyasastra*, the eyes track the hand/arm movements—an important point to note is that the eyes (vision) are not focused on the hands—they are not absorbed in observing the physical shape of the hand, they are not stimulated by the *hasta mudra* that the hand is depicting. While there is sight and awareness of space, the eyes simply follow the trajectory of the hand/arm movements. Per the *Natyasastra*, where the hand goes and the eyes follow, the mind goes there. Implying that by occupying the eyes, and not stimulating their vision by the physical image of the hand, the dancer's mind becomes engaged. The dancer's attention is thus engaged in the dance movements— *nritta*. The dancer is absorbed by and in the movement.

My experience of *nritta* suggests that while the eyes are tracking arm movements, there is slowing down of thinking process—the distractions become minimized—there is a quieter and calmer mental space that emerges. While present, it is not vacant and disengaged—instead it is completely absorbed without a thinking process present.

An interesting point to note is that the eyes stay open throughout—there is vision and awareness of physical space, but attention is not on it. The attention and concentration is on the movement being danced. In *Bharatha Natyam*, this is the embodiment of *pratyahara*. *Bharatha Natyam* facilitates this inward absorption even while the eyes stay open. This use of *nritta* in facilitating concentration represents the integrated practice of the *bahiranga* of *asana* and *pranayama* that is predicated on *dharana*.

Prayoga of Mudra

Literature review that was previously discussed suggests that in *hata* yoga, *laya* yoga and kundalini *yoga*, *mudra* are used as seals to close orifices (*banda*), or to energize pranic flow (*pranotthana*) towards an enhanced experience of Yogic communion. Some believe that in yoga (and Ayurveda), *mudra* represent the five elements of fire, air, ether, earth and water and when the fingertips are brought together in different position, "they liberate the energy locked within the body" (Menen, 2004, p. 11). The later yoga texts offer explanations on how the liberated energy flows through the body contained in *nadi* (energy channels) and when the flow is unimpeded and steady, they converge and flow upward through the central *sushumna nadi*— the "path where Eternal Grace flows" (Sovatsky, 1988, p. 2).

In *Bharatha Natyam*, *mudra* have a different stated purpose than in yoga. The *hasta mudra* as described in *Natyasastra* are used for expression (*abhinaya*) when performed in expressive dance (*nritya*) and do not have an expressive purpose when used in movement (*nritta*). A use (*prayoga*) of *mudra* is to convey the meanings of the lyrics and to express the emotions experienced by the dancer/character. Another possibility for further exploration is that *mudra* may also serve to amplify the emotional experience of the dancer by re-energizing in a recursive pattern. As a dancer expresses the experience through *mudra*, the experience is intensified as a result of using *mudra*. The various positions of holding the fingertips together (e.g., *Katakamuka*), pressing a fingertip against another finger (e.g., *bramari*), etc. may also cause an enhanced re-experience of the emotion by the dancer which is once again conveyed to the audience through the expressive *mudra*. As this process of *abhinaya* builds, so too does the experience of the dancer and the audience. This aspect of considering both uses (*prayoga*) of *hasta mudra* holds significant potential for future research.

Prayoga of Nritta

In *nritta*, there is an emphasis on feet position and percussive stamping. The feet can be stamped percussively while flat so that the entire foot comes into contact with the ground; the heel can be placed with force on the ground holding the rest of the foot upright; and, the foot can be held upright while resting firmly on the balls of the feet at the base of the toes. One foot is typically held in place under the body to ensure stability and balance while the other foot/leg can be extended to the front, side, behind or around the other foot. When the feet are moved into various positions, a rhythm emerges. In practice, the movements are danced to rhythmic beats, and the dancer's attention is on synchronizing dancing to rhythmic prompts in music.

My personal experience with feet/leg movements in *nritta* is that the percussive stamping of the feet align internal energy flow through release, stretching and movement of the lower body. When *nritta* only uses lower body, the arms are held at the waist and eyes look straight ahead—there is no effort to hold attention or turn it inwards. The eyes look at an imaginary fixed point straight ahead, as if focusing on a central point that's at eye level. In *Bharatha Natyam*, arms are used as an enhancement to leg/feet movements. The only time arms/hands are used independent of rhythmic leg movements is in their use (*prayoga*) in expressive dance. The arm movements are typically fluid while precise and the legs movements are usually rhythmic with percussive feet.

Earlier, we discussed literature that suggests that *asana* practice of postures in *hata yoga* balanced, energized and harmonized internal physical energy. One of the suggestions on how this came about was based on the *nadi* system in the body. The body was described as containing several energy channels running along and across the body, permeating all parts. When a

Yogi practices *asana*, the flow of energy is unimpeded, and regulated.

In *Bharatha Natyam*, *nritta* and for that matter, even *nritya* (also written as *nrithya*) may also be a practice whereby the internal energy flow is regulated and balanced within the body. Physical exercises, be it systematized or spontaneous suggests an effect on the energizing of the body. However, further studying of this aspect of energy flow through *nadi* and identifying their network in the body may hold significant potential.

Pranayama

Bharatha Natyam is often, an aerobic practice. While there is no deliberate regulation of breath, in order to move the body in varying rhythm and speed, there is an automatic acceleration and moderation of breathing. The acceleration follows a pattern that corresponds to the *nritta* pattern. Since the attention is engaged and directed inward, the dancer's entire awareness is on the entirety of the movement. Breathing is automatic, spontaneous and responsive to the dancing. This is consistent with the fourth level of *pranayama*.

As a research exercise, I danced while focusing my attention on my breathing—to explore what my experience was—when I did this. When I shifted my attention to breathing, I noticed it was irregular—at times out of breath and at times shallow. The moment I became aware of this irregularity, the breathing changed immediately as if reflecting my awareness. When I tried to regulate it by taking deep breaths to decelerate my breathing pattern, I felt the quality of my concentration had changed. I was no longer attentive to my movements and more importantly, this shift in attention had compromised the integration of dancing. I had lost my sense of complete immersion in the synchrony with music. My eyes were no longer tracking my arm movements, simply because my head could not move freely while regulating my breath. I was holding my head straight and not engaging with my arm movements.

When I became aware of this, I continued to stay attentive to my breath but stopped regulating it. I allowed my eyes and head to move freely as I reconnected with my dancing. Somewhere in this process of reintegrating my dance, my attention shifted away from breathing and I reclaimed focus on the entirety of movement.

At another instance, I shifted awareness to my breathing was after a fast paced rhythmic *nritta* sequence that was about 3 minutes long. As I finished the sequence and walked backwards to center myself in the physical dancing space, I became aware of my fast breathing. I was sweating and was out of breath. My body was regulating its breathing to regain its natural equilibrium. I also was aware that mentally, I was preparing myself to dance the next set of aerobic and fast paced movements. In this instance, I did not stay attentive to my breathing but slipped back into my concentration on integrated synchrony.

A related point to note here is that this type of research is representative of an aspect of arts based research, where the artist uses art as the research material, and not just as an expressive tool for depiction. The earlier video documentary demonstrated both elements of artistic exploration as a dancer/researcher; and a depiction of the experience along with a narrative describing my experience.

My experimenting with breathing regulation while dancing suggests that it detracts from the intensity and depth of concentration and reflects on the compromised integration of dance movements. This prompted my introspection on concentration (*dharana*).

Dharana

What was my concentration on? While dancing *nritta* my movements (feet, arms, and eyes) were integrated and synchronized with the music—rhythm and melody. My feet kept time with the rhythm that was reflected in precise body movements, emphasized by my eyes. My waist and arms responded to the melody in their fluid movements. However, my attention is not entirely dedicated to what I am hearing.

As another research exercise, I danced paying close and complete attention on the sounds of the music. While I was aware of some nuances I had not picked up before—overall my integration was compromised as was my immersion in dancing. In many ways, while my ears sensed the music and as I heard it, the level of my auditory engagement was somewhat similar to how my eyes were engaged in dancing.

I heard the music, but my attention was not on the music—it was on synchronizing with the musical energy of rhythm and melody. My concentration was on the synchronized integration of music and dancing. Even while I use the word concentration, I realize it suggests intensity of focus and dedicated energy.

However, this is not what concentration feels like in dancing. While there is focus, it is effortless. While there is intensity, it is also expansive. While there is attention, there is also inclusivity. It feels like being present, and aware—yet, not interfering with the process. It feels like there is a part that is aware of the physical space, aware of synchrony with music, aware of stage position, aware of mistakes being made, etc. And simultaneously, there is a part (same or another) that is absorbed, involved, engaged and immersed in the dancing. This dancing part seems to be present in the process of experiencing the dancing. The other aware part seems to regulate and correct when needed. The balance between these two aspects (self) shifts while dancing. Both are simultaneously present, at times quiet, but always alert. While dancing with others as a group or as a duo, the attentive part that is responsive to physical positioning, correcting emergent errors, etc. often has more of an active role since there is an increased need for responsive action to ensure larger harmony of the dancing, as a presentation of more than one dancer.

Pratyahara

This shifting balance between the observing self and experiencing self is representative of the intense focus of concentration expanding to meditative immersion. This is also suggestive of the dancer's sensory responses becoming engaged internally and contained in their response to external stimulus. While the eyes continue to stay open and see, the attention is not dedicated or engaged to what is seen. However, in instances when a response is appropriate, the observing self has the ability to become more active. For instance, if the dancer moves too close to the audience and at the edges of the stage, the dancer will move back to a more suitable spot of the stage. Or, if the ears register that there is a mistake that was made, the dancer will correct movements and regain synchrony with the music. Once these adjustments are made, the experiencing self regains the active role and immerses itself in the experience of the dancing process.

This state where the experiencing dancing self is stimulated only by internal processes is representative of *pratyahara*. There is a simultaneous presence (even if not active—it is alert) of an observing self that is ready to act and respond to external stimulus, at appropriate moments in time.

Vyasa in his commentary has suggested a vibrational element (*sabda*) in *pratyahara* (Narayanan, 2009, p. 58). *Natyasastra* while describing *vacika abhinaya* (spoken expression) states that the sound of words (*sabda*) "is at the source (root) of everything" (Rangacharya, 1986, p. 78). This source (*sabda*) is itself a manifestation of causal sound (*nada*) which is also the source of the phenomenal world of images and sound (Dey, 1990).

Nada is the potential or cause for audible and inaudible vibrations—it is described as causal sound (Dey, 1990, p. 6). The word *nada* means "sound" ; its related word *nadi* means "river" suggesting a flow; *nadi* is also used to mean a stream of consciousness, a meaning that goes back thousands of years to the *Rig Veda* (Berendt, 1983, pp. 15–16). The word Nada refers to sound that occurs in four dimensions, relating to frequency, degree of fineness and strength (Avalon, 1974). In the context of music as a manifestation of *nada*, Dey (1990) suggests the four dimensions are:

- *Vaikari*—is the coarsest and audible sound that can be physical produced and spoken.
- *Madhyama*—is finer than *vaikari* and can be barely heard (e.g., sound of a whisper).
- *Pashyanti*—sound that can be visualized. It can be sensed by the mind but not heard by the physical ear (e.g., Music in a dream, shapes visualized when silently chanting or recollecting a musical tune).
- *Para*—has the highest vibration and is called a transcendent sound that is heard in non-ordinary states of consciousness.

A musician who is a *nada Yogi* intuits the potential for sound and present it as audible music through creative process that moves energy (of *nada)* from *para, pashyanti, madhyama* states to overt *vaikari* state (Ramakrishna, 2005). Music is a manifestation of (the energy of) *nada* through instrumental music and vocal singing. When a dancer resonates with this musical energy made available through music, *nada* manifests as dancing (Shringy, 2007, pp. 21–22). The external vibration/sound in music is called *ahata nada* and is distinct from *anahata nada* which is an internal experience of *nada* (Sairam, 2010, p. 74). The inner experience of *nada* pulls the attention of the senses further inwards and at this state, *Bharatha Natyam* becomes representative of *pratyahara.*

Dharana at this level of engagement is a responsive immersion in *nada* and the process of dancing. The texture of concentration changes with *pratyahara,* where the observing self becomes quieter even while alert and ready to act. The dancing self begins to immerse in the experience that emerges from surrender to the energy of *nada.* On one level, the dancer's body responds with precision to the rhythmic percussion in music.

Simultaneously, the dancer's inner response is also to the energy behind the rhythmic manifestation. This energetic communication between dancer and music energizes the dancing. It raises the question if the dancer is somehow able to connect with this energy of sound that is intuitively heard by the inner ear.

A *nada Yogi* can hear the potential (at *para* or *pashyanti*) that manifests as music. Is it possible that a *natya Yogi* hears the musical energy of *nada* not only in its overt expression at *vaikari* but also at the subtler levels of *madhyama*, pashyanti *and para*? And, is it possible that this subtle energy manifests in the physical form of dance? This possibility invites speculation of how experience is shared—how the dancer resonates with the musical energy—how the audience resonates with the dancing and musical energy—how dancing emerges as a visual -physical manifestation that is further enhanced by the emotional resonance between music (musician), dance (dancer) and audience.

8. DANCING IN THE MIDDLE: EXPERIENCE IN BHARATHA NATYAM

Rasa and Samadhi

The form of *ashta anga yoga* includes physical aspects such as *asana* and *pranayama* leading to subtler inner experience of meditative immersion in *dhyana* and *samadhi*. The doorway that links the external form with its internal experience is concentration (*dharana*) as evidenced by inward engagement (*pratyahara*) of attention. Similarly, the form of *Bharatha Natyam* includes body movements (*nritta*) and expressions (*abhinaya*) that create its subtle inner experience (*rasa*). The individual *anga* of *asana, pranayama, pratyahara* and *dharana* are integrated in the practice of dancing. This chapter is dedicated to describing and understanding how the experience of dance (*rasa*) compares with the meditative experience of *ashta anga yoga* (*dhyana* and *samadhi*).

My experience of dancing—my *rasa*—is one of immersion, intermingled with its awareness. During the process of dancing, the balance and emphasis shifts between the experiencing (immersed) self and the observing (aware) self. When performing movement (*nritta*), while immersion may also be present, the emphasis is often on artistry and technique to demonstrate synchrony and rhythmic competence. The rhythmic aspect of music also acts as a magnet to shift attention inward, even as it stimulates the dancer's body with an internal experience of its vibrations. The melody in music quiets the distractions of the mind, and evokes *rasa* once synchrony between dancer and musical energy becomes established. In this state of integration, the experience of dancing shifts into an immersive stage of oneness.

In *Bharatha Natyam*, the emphasis is on emotion (*bhava*) of the music. The dancer's role as a performer is to convey the meaning and emotions of the song to the audience. The dancer's body synchronizes to this emotion allowing the dancer to step into the experiential world of the character. The artistry and techniques of expression communicate the dancer's experience to the audience. Select audience members resonate with the dancing and experience *rasa*. The *bhava* (emotion) is experienced as *rasa* by the musicians, dancer and audience and each person may have an unique experience.

Love is the dominant emotion in the music that accompanies *Bharatha Natyam*. Some dances emphasize devotional love (*bhakti*) while others depict romantic love that evokes *sringara rasa*. Separation from the beloved is the experience of love's absence and involves emotions of dejection, sadness, suspicion of infidelity, jealousy, anger, etc. Presence of love involves emotions of happiness, joy, pleasure, etc. The majority of dances are focused on some aspect of love—frequently, *samyama* in *Bharatha Natyam* is on the emotion of love.

Some dancers believe that *sringara* is the basis for all other *rasa* and is more than a romantic love—it really represents the love of a human for the Other (Narayanan, 1994, p. 19). For instance, *sringara* can be love between man and woman, or that felt by a parent for their child (*vatsalya)* or *bhakti* (devotional love) (Narayanan, 1994, pp. 33–34). Through the songs, a dancer learns about love and by dancing knows the emotion of love. Experience of self has been described as the experience of ecstasy, joy and bliss while Abhinavagupta suggests that the nature of self is serenity and its experience is one of tranquility and calmness (*shanta rasa*) (Gnoli, 1968). While *shanta rasa* is an experience of tranquility it is also considered the underpinning for all other manifestations of *rasa*. *Rasa* is the 'tasting' of one's own consciousness and one's own essential beatitude (Gnoli, 1968, p. 72). Swami Sivananda goes a step further and writes that "God is *Rasa* or essence" and one can "get eternal bliss by attainment of *rasa*" (1970, p. 24).

Knowing oneness of self (*Jiva*) and Other (*Brahman*) is the "ultimate import" of several world philosophies such as Vedanta (Sivananda, 1970). In *Bharatha Natyam,* dancers are afforded the privilege of interacting with the Other in a dialogue that serves to bring out the nature of interactions between self and Other. The dancer thereby establish a "personal relationship" with the other— the Beloved (Coomaraswamy, 1985, p. 24). While dancing the emotion of love, at times the experience of love is tempered by its other flavors such as jealousy, rejection, or longing. At such moments while immersed in the emotional dance of love, such flavors become depicted as the dominant theme. While such dances may seem like emotional experience of anger or jealousy, my experience is that it is about love—either its presence or absence. These two faces of love—togetherness and separation are suggestive of the distance between lovers, which is expressed as longing to be together or joy in oneness.

While absorbed in oneness, my experience is almost entirely immersive. However even in these instances, my experience suggests that there is a presence of an alert, even if quiet observing self. It is the presence of an observing self that allows for retrospective integration of the immersion. This co-existence of the experiencing (immersed) self and the observing (aware) self is what allows a dancer to both immerse and later, relish the immersion.

This chapter undertakes an exploration into the interactional experience between these two aspects that is my dancing *rasa*—the experience (immersion), and its experiencing (awareness). Concurrently, the exploration includes how *rasa* may correspond to the meditative immersion of *samyama* with focus on the continuum of *dhyana* leading to *samapati* and *samadhi*.

During *samadhi* and *rasa*, the two aspects of immersion and awareness seem to be co-exist, albeit at shifting levels of activity. While immersed in *samadhi* the awareness is quiet and it is later, that there is integration and recognition of the intuitive knowing that arises while immersed in *samadhi*. In the context of *rasa*, while immersed in an emotion, the awareness of this immersion can come during or after. If it emerges during the immersion, it can interfere and reflect on the depth and intensity of immersion and thereby compromise its experience. While my experience suggests that this straddling of two aspects (awareness and immersion) certainly happens in dancing, textual analysis of *samadhi* suggests that a similar co-existence of observing and experiencing self may also hold true for other meditative practices of yoga. Literature review of yoga suggests that, dedicated focus (*dharana*) and meditative immersion (*dhyana*) through a process of *samyama* leads to knowledge (*prajnya*). *Samyama* on specific objects leads to *prajnya* that corresponds to that object (Feuerstein, 1989). While *prajnya* emerges while immersed in the *samadhi* of oneness, awareness and cognition happens when the active mind emerges (Kripalvananda, 1977).

Dhyana is the state of meditative immersion that involves progressive submersion of the observing self in the experiencing self, until finally all that remains is oneness of experience and experiencing self. During such a state of samadhi, intuitive knowledge or *prajnya* arises. This knowledge (*prajnya*) when acquired through *samyama* on words is *savitarka samapati*;

without verbal thinking is *nirvitarka samapati*; conditioned in time and space is *savicara samapati*; beyond this conditioning by time and space is *nirvicara samapati* (Mukherji, 1981, pp. 92–98). However, C. R. Narayanan (personal communication, February 7, 2012) suggested that *savicara* and *nirvicara* are attributes that describe the reflective ability of a Yogi that act as additional descriptors for *savitarka* and *nirvitarka samapati*.

The power of *samadhi* is such that while in the presence of a great Yogi, like Ramakrishna Paramahamsa, it is stated that even an engaged audience experienced *samadhi* (Nikhilananda, 1988, p. 435). As a dancer and performer, I interpret this as a receptive and engaged audience that resonates with the energy of depiction. In the context of *Bharatha Natyam*, such an audience member is called *sahrdaya* and is described as possessing a "clean heart" that reflects what is depicted on stage; having a capacity to "become one" with the experience presented; and having an ability to experience the emotion in the "poet's heart" when the words emerged (Deshpande, 1989, p. 87). A *sahrdaya* is a sensitive and sympathetic spectator (Shah, 2003, p. 154). The two "pre-conditions" for "rasa realization" are *hrdayasamvad* (resonance of the heart) and *thanmayibhavan* (complete immersion with sustained experience) (Pande, 2009, p. xxii). In the immersed realization of *rasa,* the aesthete (the experiencer of aesthetic experience) goes beyond a ego centric experience and this state is comparable to *samadhi* wherein a feeling of oneness emerges.

This immersive oneness experienced in *rasa* appears consistent with the corresponding meditative state in *samadhi*. An awareness of this immersion may alter the experience of complete oneness but not necessarily dispel it. In dancing, my immersion in an emotion co-exists with the presence of an observing self, which is later able to recollect, re-experience and savor the immersive state of oneness. There have been times when the observing self becomes more active, interfering with the ability to stay immersed in the experience. This can happen as a response to the changing musical prompts, physical surroundings, dancer's physical discomfort or mental distractions. While it is possible to reverse this interruption, it also suggests that in a state of immersive oneness, the observing self is present while quiet and not active. This experience (*rasa*) of immersion in oneness is consistent with *samadhi,* where the "I" is not active and is immersed in a state of oneness with the original object of focused attention. The *prajnya* that results from such *samadhi* is realized only with the re-emergence of the "I" or the observing self. Both *rasa* and *samadhi* appear to be terms for experience of oneness, by a self with another.

Gnoli suggests that the creative or artistic intuition (knowledge) is borne from an expression of feeling or passion that is free from constraints of "time and space" (1968). In the foreword, Vatsyayan compliments leading *abhinaya* exponent, Kalanidhi Narayanan's dancing ability in moving freely in time accessing emotional memory "of time past, of time present, and time future" (Narayanan,1994).

Rasa in Alaripu

While dancing the *Alaripu*, (as narrated), I was aware of the physical constraints of the dancing space, my position in relation to the camera, wondering if this would re-create or enact a realistic dance experience for the viewer, and so on. My attention was split unequally between the experiencing self and the observing self, with the latter more active. Even while aware of the distractions, through the process of dancing my body was calibrating itself towards a recollected balance and synchrony within and with music.

This dance is representative of *nritta* that does not have an expressive purpose in *natya*. In the context of performing, it is the introductory dance that presents the dancer to the audience and vice versa. It is the first dance that invites the dancer to sense the physical dancing hall (while dancing) that is now inclusive of the individual and collective energies of the audience. It is the first dance that the dancer attempts synchrony with the music, even as the musicians are going through their own individual and collective process of synchrony with music, audience and dancer.

In the context of *ashta anga*, this *nritta* is representative of the combined elements of *asana* and *pranayama* with an emerging *dharana*. In the context of *rasa*, *nritta* paves the way for a dancer to balance self energy (physical and mental) in preparation to synchronize more fully with the external energy of music. The synchrony with music is present throughout dancing, but at this initial stage, dancing is responsive to rhythm and follows the musical prompts working towards a more complete integration with music.

Rasa in Jathiswaram

My experience dancing *Jathiswaram* was an increased appreciation of melody, as it expressed itself through my body movements. My experience was one of synchrony expressed by the rhythm of my feet and the percussive drumming in music. I was less conscious (perhaps less aware, too) of the physical surroundings—less concerned about expression and audience engagement—less responsive to the external stimulus of space.

The word *Jathiswaram* implies finding the rhythmic beats (*jati*) in musical notes (*swara*). The rhythmic cycle for this dance was a seven beat (*misra*) pattern while the musical notes were combined in several melodies (*raga*). Each melodic sequence was charged in a different energy, both in their composition and the musician's rendition. When I danced to differing melodies, even while the rhythm remained constant—I found my experience of the dance movements qualitatively distinct from one another. The body's response to the melodic energy was reflective of the dance choreography and its role in communicating visually the musical movement in the melody.

The audience heard the musical movement and saw the dance depiction of the same movement. There were two expressions of the melodic energy in music. There were at least two manifestations of the *Jathiswaram*—musical and dancing—auditory and visual.

Nritta in this dance while not having an overt interpretive role, was expressive of the musical movement. As far as the dancer is concerned, the synchrony and integration between dance and music was enhanced. This integration is suggestive of a higher intensity of involvement and concentration by the dancer (and musician). With regards to *ashta anga*, this stage of *nritta* is representative of an integrated practice of *asana*, *pranayama* and *dharana* with emerging *pratyahara*.

Rasa in Varnam (Nrithyopaharam)

In *Varnam* the role of the dancer is as a narrator and as character, stepping from one into the other. While in the role of the narrator, the dancer depicts rhythmic *nritta*—in the role as the character, the dancer enacts the story as an expressive narration by the character.

The singer supports the dancer's narration by rendering the lyrics in the song with an appropriate emotion (*bhava*). In return, the dancer visually depicts the emotional movement in music. The dancer understands the setting of the story, the personality and emotional state of the character (*sthayi bhava)* and with the aid of the musical energy and *bhava* is able to step into the role of the character.

When interpreting the words and developing the story, my experience is visual. I 'see' the scene that I am depicting—it is not an active or deliberate exercise that I undertake. While it is possible that with years of practice that this has become second nature to my dancing, my experience is that the visualization emerges spontaneously. What I mean is that I am aware that I am recreating a setting that is an imaginary picture of the physical entities. However, when I depict my conversation with a friend, I am utilizing the picture for information such as the eye level contact to suggest a physical height and also the friend's attention to what I am 'saying'. When I am interacting and engaged in this dialogue, I depict what the words in the song say, and I dance with the emotions of the character's *sthayibhava*. When the depiction is not limited by words and I am dancing to convey the emotions, my *sancari bhava* (*vyabhichari bhava*) builds on the emotional energy (*bhava*) from the music and my own intuited understanding of the emotion.

When dancing *nritta*, my experience is one of immersion in the melody and rhythm. There is an active awareness of synchrony that is co-present. This balance between my observing and immersed self, shifts when engaged in emotional expression. While expressing the emotions of the character, I am aware of my role as interpretive storyteller. My observing self becomes quiet and is present to the evolving dance. With regards to *ashta anga* while dancing *nritta* in Varnam, *Bharatha Natyam* is representative of an integrated practice of *asana, pranayama* with increasing focus (*dharana*) and immersion (*dhyana*). While engaging in expressive and experiential dialogue, *Bharatha Natyam* is additionally representative of emerging states of *dhyana* where the focus is on synchrony and communicating the message of the music. While dancing the interpretive content, the *abhinaya* is representative of meditative immersion of *dhyana*—it is only when there is emphasis on *sancari bhava* that the *abhinaya* becomes more immersed in the emotion focused upon and it is at this stage that there is a glimpse of *samapati*. The interactive dialogue while immersed in experience has aspects of vocal music, latent thoughts, and implied reasoning—and may be suggestive of a brief and tentative foray into *savitarka samapati* or even *nirvitarka samapati*.

Rasa in Javali

The next three dances that are depicted and discussed emphasize the emotional experience aspect of *Bharatha Natyam*. The dancer at this stage has established a sound connection with the energy of music and dancing is synchronized with music. Next, the dancer moves beyond the overt expression of words in the song, and depicts the meaning behind the words. The focus is on experiencing the character's emotional state in an authentic manner so that it expresses naturally and audience resonate with the depicted experience.

My experience of dancing the *Javali* was initially twofold—I wanted to establish the *sthayi bhava* of the character for the audience to understand the context of the dance; and, it also facilitated my process of stepping into the character's experience. This initial prelude helped develop a deep grounding in the character's frame of mind at that moment. Initial interpretations of the words were from this perspective. And soon, the transition was into the meaning behind the words—what was not said by the words, but intended by the words. The depiction (*abhinaya*) was to present the true meaning of the dialogue that went beyond its overt expression.

My experience was mixed emotions—still bound by latent thoughts, suggestive reasoning and impressions of mental processes of "how could this happen to me?" while in the role of the character. I felt the dialogue and the engagement of the other, once again visualized the energy behind the interactions that manifested as my *abhinaya* of the emotion (*bhava*). At this stage, *Bharatha Natyam* is representative of the *anga* up to *dhyana* leading into *samapati*. Depending on the precise moment in the dance, the engrossment and immersion in the emotion can hover around *savitarka/nirvitarka (savicara/nirvicara) samapati*.

Rasa in Padam

In this *Padam*, the emotion focused upon is devotional love, *bhakti*. The *samyama* on *bhakti* creates an experiential knowing of complete self-surrender in *bhakti*. It expresses as fervent and earnest longing for divine blessings—in this case the gift of dance. The recollection of a previous experience intensified this re-experience of *bhakti*. There was minimal awareness of interpretive responsibility as a dancer and dedicated immersion in the emotional experience of *bhakti*.

My *rasa* was of completely surrender and being enveloped in and by the emotional energy of *bhakti*. My attunement was to the emotional energy (*bhava*) of the singing—my resonance was with the energy behind the words and its rendition. My visualization was dancing at the temple in Chidambaram facing the idol of

Nataraja—the Cosmic dancer. Some parts of the visualization are from my memory. But my re-experience was different—it was renewed with my increased understanding over the past 20 years since I had danced there. As a dancer, my depiction was different; as a devotee my experience was textured different; the essence of *bhakti* was similar but experienced differently now than it was 20 years ago.

My experience of *bhakti* appears consistent with description of *ananda* and at its most intense experience, it was only *bhakti* that remained—the "I" had been subsumed within the emotion of *bhakti*, even if only for a moment. At those moments, *rasa* may be suggestive of *asmita* even while the entire experience is an embodied one, and possible only with the benefit of a physical "I."

Rasa in Ashtapadhi

My *samyama* was on love and the emerging experience was one of knowing love. The experience was not verbal, not responsive to the words of the song—primarily because it was not a language I spoke. While this was also true of the *Javali*, in this dance, my resonance was with the soulful music and the energy it represented. My response was the emotion it evoked and elicited— while my dance expressed this emotion, it was simultaneous as my experience of it. I was not concerned about the expression or interpretive responsibility. My observing self was invisible in its presence. My articulation of the experience came later. My cumulative and collective knowing of love enriched and enhanced each experience of the emotion.

There were moments especially while in the throes of longing, that there was nothing but emotion, similar to when I experienced *bhakti*. At these moments, *Bharatha Natyam* is clearly representative of straddling immersion and dissolution; *dhyana* and *samadhi*.

One point to dwell on further is the description of *dharana* in the context of *Bharatha Natyam*. If the concentration is not on a object or sense organ, but instead on the potential of an emotion that is suggested, is this sort of concentration representative of *sabija* (with seed) or *nirbija* (without seed)? The dancer does not set out with focus on an internal or external entity. The dancer surrenders to the process and energy of dancing, almost stepping out its way. If dancing emerges as a result of the self stepping out of the way, then there is no self that is active in the process of concentration. There is only an experiencing active self engaged in dancing and being danced. If one were to consider this as a possibility, then the path of meditative immersion in *Bharatha Natyam* is possibly equivalent to *nirbija samadhi*.

Rasa and Samadhi

As an experiment, I worked with musicians who had an intuitive musical ear. We collaborated in creating music that synthesized specific melodies that had traditionally been shown to evoke certain *rasa*. We did not consciously compose the rhythmic component but instead allowed it to emerge in response to the *rasa* that the melodies evoked. We deliberately did not use words or vocal music to express emotion. I choreographed a vignette around human emotions of excited anticipation, disappointment, sorrow, anger, and surrender. I had a tentative flow in mind when the music was composed. While my training and dancing language is *Bharatha Natyam*, I did not choreograph dance sequences to express anything—I did not have a script of *mudra* or expressions that I had created. The focus was on exploring how musical energy and specific *raga* evoked a corresponding *rasa*; and when that experience was authentic and intense, how that emotion finds a way to express itself unrestrained by language, or form. Since the expression was through my body while in the role of a dancer, the form was recognizable as Indian dance but did not have rhythmic movements (*nritta*) or expressive form (*nritya*). I was able to truly experience immersion without a strict form to maintain.

Arts Based Depiction

Please view the video playlist titled *Rasa* in *Bharatha Natya Yoga.*

http://natyayogatherapy.net/bharathanatyayoga/

While dancing, I found a qualitative difference between emotions—the intense experience that seemed to transcend "I" was while knowing the emotion of longing and joy. While knowing the emotion of longing, all that was present was the heaviness and emotion of longing—I could later describe it with words of sorrow, rejection, depressed mood, pain, etc. but my experience at that moment was oneness with that energy (that I now describe as longing). At the time, it was only the energy—intense, powerful, heavy, strong with an unbearable presence and weight. It was expressed in dance as dejection and pain from the unrequited love and longing for the other.

Similarly, when experiencing union with the other, I now describe the emotion as happiness and joy, through surrender. At the time, there was only the emotion—no description. This emotion was lighter, bouncier, energizing, moving and dynamic. It expressed itself in dance as joy and bliss in union with the other.

While in other states, there was a co-existing awareness and dialogue more indicative of stages of *samapati*. But while in the states of longing and joy, there was only the emotional energy. However, right through this process, my focus was not on any emotion. As dancer, I was simply present and open to dancing. If we consider that these moments, there is no object of focus, *samyama* is not attached to any entity, then the resulting experience may be comparable to *nirbija samadhi*. On the other hand, since emotion was the intuitive knowing (*prajnya*), the *samyama* may be on the emotion and creative energy in music (*nada*) that manifests as *rasa*.

Rasa in Thillana (Nrittangaharam)

My experience of the *thillana* is the re-emergence and separation of my observing self from the experiencing self. Rhythm invites, creates and consolidates this separation for dancer and potentially for audience. Rhythmic precision demands concentration and focus away from the emotions of the melodic song. It shifts attention towards the physical depiction and synchrony with percussion and rhythm in music.

I experienced the initial transition as a distinct shift in *samyama*, which creates a path that leads out of the immersed state of oneness. This path seems different from the *samapati* (also written as *samapatti*) state where the meditative immersion is increasing in intensity and depth. This path of re-emergence seems to re-establish the prominence of the observing self, as if preparing for engagement with external sensory stimulation. The *thillana* wraps up the dancing experience and segues into real life interactions. The intensity and prolonged engagement transforms dancer and audience.

This aspect of audience experience has been called *rasa* by several commentators. The dancer's role is to stimulate such receptive audience members (*sahrdaya*) who are able to resonate and experience *rasa* that is evoked by music and dance. While this aspect is not the focus of this study, audience response to participatory *Natya Yoga* holds potential for further studies to explore how this experience is created and facilitated in *natya*.

The presence of an involved audience and an appreciative experience plays an important role in the overall experience of dancing. This aspect of the interactions between dancer and audience in the co-creation of an unitive experience holds potential for future research. While rehearsing, the presence of even one engaged viewer can have an impact on the quality of experience for the dancer. My experience is that dancing in another's presence enhances my own dancing and its experience.

Dancing creates a meditative experience for the dancer and the audience. The capacity to evoke the healing experience of meditation through *natya* holds tremendous potential for future research, especially its use as a therapeutic modality to stimulate healing through creative arts. Exploring the role of a dancer not only as a *Yogi* but also as a healer holds significant promise of expanding and integrating the disciplines of psychotherapy and arts.

Further studies on using movement as a path to meditation could offer increased options for individuals who are unable to quiet their mind using other meditative practices. With regards to its therapeutic value, as a psychotherapist it excites me to consider the efficacy of meditation in movement for clients diagnosed with symptoms of anxiety, who are unable to directly control their mental agitation. Accessing their body through physical movement that also engages their mind may allow an easier integration of their internal energies and mind-body connections.

9. RE-VISION OF BHARATHA NATYAM AS NATYA YOGA

The language of *ashta anga yoga* offered a vocabulary to understand how the external form of *Bharatha Natyam* leads to its inner experience, *rasa*. While the literature on dance suggests that *rasa* was commonly understood as an experiencing of an external essence, my engagement in the narrative and arts based study of *rasa* leads me to suggest that *rasa* is also an experience without an external factor. In the context of dance an audience viewing the dancer may experience the dance as their *rasa*. A musician may enjoy the music as an external *rasa* to the song that is heard and also as an internal *rasa* of the music. A dancer does not have the luxury of visual experience of her dancing. Her experience is internal—her *rasa* of dancing is not by external senses—it is an inner experience. The inner or external factor that evokes *rasa* does not change the understanding of the word, *rasa*. I understand *rasa* as an inner experience of a dancer, musician and audience. The individual nature of experience differs from person to person and some perspectives (such as audience experience) may be better represented than others. However, a dancer's experience of dancing is consistent with the understanding of *rasa* as an essence that is experienced.

Previous chapters described how the form of *Bharatha Natyam* was an embodiment of the external form (*bahiranga*) of *ashta anga yoga* that led to its inner experience (*antaranga*). In *Bharatha Natyam*, the inner experience is called *rasa* and in *ashta anga yoga*, the inner experience of meditative immersion is described as *dhyana* leading into *samadhi*. This final chapter outlines how my study re-visions *Bharatha Natyam* as *Natya Yoga*.

Rasa is Experience of Oneness

In *Bharatha Natyam*, *rasa* is usually experience of an emotion. There are two interrelated parts to this experience—immersion and awareness. In the immersed state, a dancer can become one with the emotion and know the emotion as an embodied experience. And, for a dancer to become aware of the immersion there is a separation that is suggested from this meditative immersion. Even while immersed in the emotional experience, an observing part is ever present, in a quiet yet alert state. It is the presence of this observing self that allows a dancer to integrate the experiential knowing of an emotion.

Reading about the stages of *samadhi* and *samapati*, I understand these concepts much the same way. As meditation intensifies, *dhyana* develops into *samadhi* as the immersive experience transcends cognitive knowing of the object focused upon. At a state when the Yogi becomes one with the object, *prajnya* emerges—this state is *samprajnyata samadhi*. In this immersed state, while the intuitive knowledge of *prajnya* cannot be recognized without the emergence of the observing self, it also suggests a coexisting presence of this observing self. Said differently, the observing self has to coexist even while the *Yogi* is immersed in *samadhi* for cognition of *prajnya*.

The coexisting presence of an observing self even in the immersed state is the state of oneness that is described in *ashta anga yoga* as *samadhi* and is experienced in *natya* as *rasa*. *Samadhi* is an experiential state that is the goal of *ashta anga* yoga while *rasa* is the experience that is the goal of natya. In *natya* the dancer and audience both experience *rasa*. In the context of an emotional experience, *rasa* is an experience of oneness between experiencer, experience and experienced. The state of oneness includes the immersion in the emotion and its coexisting awareness that allows for later savoring of the entire experience.

Re-Claim Rasa as Purpose of Natya

Chapter 5 synthesized hermeneutic interpretations of the *Natyasastra* that reiterated that the purpose of *natya* is to evoke *rasa*. The dancer's inner experience of dancing, *rasa* was explored in Chapters 4, 7, and 8. Chapter 2 presented literature review that suggested that *natya* was the predecessor of Indian classical dance forms that later transformed into present day forms of *Kathak, Kuchipudi, Odissi, Mohini Attam*, etc.. Each of these styles adapted to prevailing socio-cultural influences and their attire, form, content changed accordingly. In this evolutionary process the shared essence of *rasa* may have become less represented in each dance form. While the various styles of Indian classical dance still include *hasta mudra, bhava, abhinaya*, and *rasa* there is relatively less importance that is placed on *rasa* as the purpose of *natya*. This study re-presents to all *natya* the shared commonality of *rasa* that is the essence of Indian classical dance forms. This study was based on dance forms like *Bharatha Natyam* that trace their origin to *natya* that is described in the *Natyasastra*. However, this essence of dancing experience, *rasa* may not be unique or exclusive to Indian dancing. It is possible that it might also extend to other world dances. This is an area for further studies, especially by dancers trained in other world dance traditions.

Re-Define Purpose of Nritta in Natya

Chapter 5 posed a question as to the purpose of *nritta* in *natya*. In keeping with the dictates of the *Natyasastra, nritta* (movement) may have little interpretive purpose—but my experience suggests that *nritta* does express a dancer's engagement with music and movement. The beauty and grace of *nritta* adds aesthetic value to dance and the performance. It demonstrates an integration and synchrony between the energy of music and dancing. A dancer who is not synchronized with music may not be able to depict the movement and grace of the melody. She may not be able to demonstrate the precise synchrony in rhythms. Such a depiction of *nritta* expresses a dancer's incompatibility with music and self while also creating a discordant and jarring note for the audience.

The physical aspect of *nritta* serves to align the dancer's body to ensure balance and unimpeded movement of inner energies. *Nritta* integrates the eyes, arms, legs and torso of the body and synchronizes the body. It may have a similar role to that of *asana* in *ashta anga yoga*. Both practices may settle the body's energy and prepare the dancer for a higher level of integrated and meditative experience. Just as *asana* prepares a *Yogi* to enter *dhyana*, *nritta* prepares a dancer (and perhaps, even audience) for *rasa*.

As far as a dancer is concerned, if there are physical or mental distractions, a dancer's ability to move into an immersive experience is compromised. *Nritta* facilitates this immersive experience of *rasa* by settling the energies inside the body harmoniously. The process by which *nritta* accomplishes this balancing may be an area worthy of further exploration.

Similarly, *nritta* may also serve to settle the energies of an audience group and channel their attention towards a dancer. As an audience member I have experienced physical relaxation watching a dance performance. I have experienced mental calmness from watching a dance presentation. The ability of *nritta* to engage the audience on a multisensory level is one worthy of further exploration.

Re-Integrate Necessity of Oneness in Natya

The dancer would need to feel the emotion prior to its communication to the audience. This process by which a dancer develops the ability to resonate with emotions and experiences is not described in the *Natyasastra*. The ability to know an emotion and experience it authentically is a prerequisite to expressing it in dancing. While dancing is also the process that facilitates the knowing, this process is better captured while using the vocabulary and language of *ashta anga yoga*. The *Yogasutra* describes the knowing that emerges in *samadhi* as *prajnya*. In *Bharatha Natyam, prajnya* emerges while the dancer is immersed in the emotional experience of dancing. It is this experience of oneness that allows a dancer to know the emotional experience. This oneness allows a dancer to authentically experience the emotion that is then to be communicated to the audience.

This aspect of oneness between dancer and dance is not clearly represented in the *Natyasastra* and the vocabulary of *ashta anga yoga* enriches understanding of this process in *natya*.

Re-Position Natyasastra as Technical Manual

When *natya* is understood as *yoga*, the *Natyasastra* positions itself as a manual that describes the techniques of communicating oneness to the audience. The audience experience of oneness is described as *rasa*, the purpose of *natya*. The *Natyasastra* describes the resonance and sensitivity to *rasa* in some audience members (*sahrdaya*) as an attribute that is cultivated by exposure to *natya* experiences. The *Natyasastra* describes body positions, hand gestures, facial expressions, etc. as tools employed by the dancer in communicating the oneness that is facilitated by dancing. Here, the practice of dancing becomes both—the facilitator of oneness, and the expression of oneness. The facilitation of oneness qualifies *Bharatha Natyam* as a practice of *yoga* while its expression and facilitation of oneness in others transform *Bharatha Natyam* into *Natya Yoga*.

Re-Vision of Bharatha Natyam as Yoga

For *natya* to transform into *yoga*, the ability to integrate the body and mind is a requirement. *Natya* is an integrated practice that facilitates this and continually improves the dancer's ability to achieve a higher state of integration. For *natya* to transform into *yoga*, its practice should lead to a meditative experience comparable to *dhyana* that can develop into *samadhi*. Emergent intuitive knowing (*prajnya*) is described as evidence of *samadhi*.

In the context of *Bharatha Natyam* since the *samyama* (focus of meditation) is emotions, the resulting intuitive knowing (*prajnya)* is emotional in nature. If the knowing that emerges in *rasa* is comparable to the intuitive knowing described in *prajnya*, it suggests that *rasa* could well be an experience of *samadhi*. My experience of *Bharatha Natyam* is that a dancer's *rasa* is an experience of oneness that is described in *yoga* as *samadhi*. My experience as an audience member watching my teacher's dancing was comparable to my own dancing experience, except I had the luxury of immersing myself in the emotion without feeling the responsibility of dancing. My experience of *rasa* as an audience member is an experience of oneness with the emotional experience of the dancer.

However, without an objective measure for *samadhi*, the correlation is more likely the natural unfolding beginning with a particular quality of experience. At present, I have not developed the competence to suggest that I know *samadhi*. Therefore prior to making the suggestion that *rasa* may be an experience of *samadhi*, it behooves us to further study their correlation both in practice and in theory. For example, a study that seeks narratives from *Yogi* and dancers on their experiences of immersion in their practice will provide a better understanding of how *samadhi* and *rasa* are experienced and allow a comparison of these two experiences.

When understood as yoga *Bharatha Natyam* transforms into a practice that is an embodiment of the *ashta anga* principles of yoga. *Yama* and *niyama* being moral observances and practices may be lifelong pursuits that can transform a dancer into a Yogi. The integrated practice of *asana* and *pranayama* is represented in *nritta*, where the focus (*dharana*) facilitates and is evidenced by complete inner engagement and withdrawal of external sensory stimulation (*pratyahara*). When this integration completes and intensifies the inner energy (*pranayama*) a meditative immersion (*dhyana*) emerges that can lead to *samadhi*. *Bharatha Natyam* is an integrated practice of *ashta anga yoga* and evokes a meditative experience comparable to *dhyana* with potential for further immersion as described in *samadhi*.

Re-Vision of Bharatha Natyam as Natya Yoga

Bharatha Natyam is representative of *natya* when it serves the purpose of evoking *rasa* in the audience. As an embodiment and practice of *ashta anga yoga*, *Bharatha Natyam* can be a self-oriented practice by a dancer for self-cultivation, self-enjoyment and self-enrichment. It can be a practice in the privacy of a dancing space, including no other but the dancer. In this setting, the practice of *Bharatha Natyam* qualifies as *ashta anga yoga*, but not as *natya*.

For a dance form to qualify as *natya*, it has to meet the purpose of *natya* that is to evoke *rasa* in the audience. When a dancer communicates the experience of oneness, *rasa*, to the audience—the dancer is effectively representing *natya* following the techniques described in the *Natyasastra*. It is only when the oneness is experienced as *rasa* by the audience that *Bharatha Natyam* transforms into *Natya Yoga*, where through the practice of *natya*, the dancer and audience experience oneness that is *yoga*. The dancer is a Yogi when she experiences oneness, *rasa*, in her dancing. A dancer is a *natya Yogi* when she is able to share her oneness through the techniques of *natya* and is able to evoke a similar state of oneness, *rasa*, in the audience.

As a dancer my experience is powerful, when performing or for that matter, rehearsing in the presence of even one receptive person. When the audience is engaged and involved in the experiencing, their participation and appreciation of dancing re-energizes my dancing. The participative presence of the audience contributes to the dancing experience, elevating the personal *rasa* of a dancer to a higher level of unitive *rasa* of dancer, dance, music, and audience. The interactive dynamics in collaborative creation and experience of dancing is a fascinating process worthy of further study.

Re-Vision Natya Yoga as an Embodiment of Selflessness

A dancer usually dedicates several years of her life to mastering the techniques of dancing. The practice shapes the form of her dance and creates in the dancer an ability to experience integration within her body. A dancer who nurtures this integrated oneness within herself becomes a *Yogi* when she is able to also connect with the pervasive metaphysical energies on the outside. At this level of experience, the dancer/Yogi feels the oneness and interconnectedness between herself and what lies outside of herself. Her work as a dancer/*Yogi* in seeking the integration, harmony and balance is perhaps done. However, her role as a representative of *natya* begins only at this point of oneness. The role of a *natya Yogi*/dancer is to share this oneness with the audience—to communicate the intensity of this experience so that another can experience the same oneness.

An audience member who is receptive to the experience of dance and is able to experience *rasa* is referred to as *sahrdaya*. Such a person is described as one who is able to resonate with the dancer, music and feel the same emotional energy experienced and expressed through dance. The creation of such an audience member, *sahrdaya*, is described as an outcome of repeated exposure to *natya*. A dancer's role is to create, nurture, and facilitate experience of oneness (*rasa*) in another. In order to accomplish this, a dancer has to first create, nurture, and facilitate the experience of oneness (*rasa*) in herself. This inbuilt practice of generosity in the practice of *natya* is to be emphasized and taken note of.

This generosity of spirit is embodied in the practice of *natya* where the outcome of oneness in the dancer is only a prerequisite for evoking the same oneness in the audience. This selfless practice in *Natya Yoga* is also an embodiment of *ashta anga yoga* that is often misrepresented and approached as a self-oriented practice.

Looking into the future

This study suggests that *Bharatha Natyam* is an embodiment of *ashta anga yoga*. The form of *Bharatha Natyam* is compared to the form of *ashta anga yoga* while its experience (*rasa*) is compared to the meditative immersion of *dhyana/samadhi*. My experiences as a dancer afford me visibility on the form of *Bharatha Natyam* leading to its experience. The *Natyasastra* describes the form and experience of *natya* but does not offer suggestions on how the form of *natya* creates its experience.

Review of the *Yogasutra* suggests that the *ashta anga yoga* describes the external form of yoga that leads to its inner meditative experience. However, it does not offer suggestions on this process of experience that is facilitated by form. In the context of *hata yoga*, the text of *Hata Yoga Pradipika* describes subtle energy that flows through channels (*nadi*) that intersect at specified centers (*chakra*) in the body.

While *asana* and *mantra* are prescribed to alleviate impeded energy flow in the body, there is minimal research on how external form and practice facilitates flow of subtle energy or how this translates into mind/body integration. Understanding how *asana* impacts the subtle energy flow in the body holds tremendous potential for its use in regulating impeded energy flow at specific points in the body. This link between subtle energy flow in *nadi* and its role in connecting external practice (*bahiranga*) with internal experience (*antaranga*) bears significant potential for future research.

In the context of *Bharatha Natyam*, understanding how various *nritta* (movement) of the body changes the energy flow can create an ability to regulate impeded energy flow in specific areas of the body, by using a corresponding movement. In *natya*, expressive gestures (*mudra*) convey the meaning of a song whereas in yoga, *mudra* seal and bind energy flow in that portion of the body. With further exploration of this aspect of *nritta* and energy flow, it is possible that *mudra* play both roles of expressing and regulating energy in the body.

The connection between unimpeded energy flow and an inner meditative experience has not yet been researched. With improved understanding of this process, a link between the external form and internal experience may emerge. The *Yogasutra* describes *ashta anga yoga* as a process of moving from external form to internal meditative experience. *Bharatha Natyam* is an integrated practice of a stylized form that creates its inner experience, *rasa*.

In the midst of such studies on form of *Bharatha Natyam* and *ashta anga yoga* practices, it is also important to gather a variety of experiences. While my experience of *Bharatha Natyam* may be unique, seeking narratives from other dancers on their experiences will add to the understanding of *rasa*. Study is also needed to further validate this study's suggestion that *rasa* is meditative immersion as described in *ashta anga yoga*. One of the limitations of this study was impoverished descriptions on the experience of *samadhi*. While it may be easier for dancers to share and describe their dancing experience, *rasa* it is also important to gather testimonies of experiences of *samadhi* within yoga and *Bharatha Natyam*.

Concurrent with further studies, it is also important to understand how this present study changes existing practice of *Bharatha Natyam*. *Bharatha Natyam* is presently practiced as an interpretive storytelling dance. When practiced as *Natya Yoga*, *Bharatha Natyam* can emphasize its meditative experience with a spontaneous healing outcome for dancer and audience. However for this to come about, dancers and dance teachers need to know what transforms *Bharatha Natyam* into Natya Yoga. A practice manual that accompanies the existing *Natyasastra* is one way to address this need. This practice manual can link the concepts described in *Natyasastra* with the practice of *natya*. A written practice manual can suggest a language which connects the practice with its concepts, and represent what may have been insofar experienced by dancers.

Toward A Natya Yoga Sastra

The *Natyasastra* describes the various techniques that comprise the form of *nritta viz.* facial expressions, hand gestures, feet positions, arm positions, etc. The *Natyasastra* also describes the essence of emotions and their expressions. While the expressions (*abhinaya*) and emotions (*bhava*) are detailed, a framework that integrates their physical form to their inner experience is not represented in the *Natyasastra*. Adding a practice manual that offers this link would be invaluable for students like me who resource the text with the benefit of an immersion in the practice of dance.

The language of *ashta anga yoga* provides a framework that is inclusive of form and experience. It would be apt to call such a practice manual *Natya Yoga Sastra* that reconciles the form and experience of *Bharatha Natyam* with a conceptual framework of *ashta anga yoga*. A chapter in the *Natya Yoga Sastra* could describe the vocabulary of *ashta anga yoga* and describe each *anga*. Chapter 6 in this book offers a contribution towards such a chapter. Another chapter in the *Natya Yoga Sastra* could describe how an external form and practice leads to its inner experience. Chapters 7 and 8 in this book may work as drafts towards making this connection in *Bharatha Natyam*. Practitioners of other Indian dance forms could also make a similar link in their practice of *natya* and add to such a practice manual for their form of dancing.

The *Natya Yoga Sastra* will allow a dancer to understand the value of movement in dance; understand the relevance of movement in evoking *rasa;* understand the purpose of *natya* and *rasa* not only as an aesthetic experience but also as a metaphysical experience. Such an integration between the artistic and spiritual dimension also brings together what may have been separated only in conceptual understandings but has remained integrated within the practice of arts.

When a dancer approaches *Bharatha Natyam* as *Natya Yoga*, the dancer's body can transform into more than a vehicle for narrating stories. It can also become a vessel for experiencing oneness. Such a dancer has the privilege of experiencing oneness and an audience watching the dancer may also become privy to experiencing *rasa* of the dancer's meditative immersion.

Prayoga of Natya Yoga as a Healing Tradition

My experience of *Bharatha Natyam* suggests that the form and structure of this dance facilitates a self-transcending experience of oneness. A dancer can experience such meditative immersion and oneness while simultaneously also sharing the experience with receptive audience members. In this context a dancer may be looked upon as a facilitator of meditative oneness, in self and the viewers.

Several indigenous healing practices suggest that an experience of oneness can act as a healing force. When a healer experiences oneness, the body then becomes a vehicle for the expression and transmission of this healing force. Healers dance to sacred songs to invite the spirits and once a connection is established, a feeling of oneness seems to emerge. In this state of oneness and immersed trance, the healer is able to act as a conduit for the healing energies that become embodied. The knowing of how to heal through herbs and other instruments can also be intuited while in this trance like state of oneness. If healing is a spontaneous outcome of a state of oneness, I wonder if *Bharatha Natyam* can be developed further to be used as a therapeutic tool to bring about healing.

As a psychotherapist, I notice that meditation is a common prescriptive treatment for symptoms of anxiety and distress from life events. However, while in this state of anxiety, the individual is not able to quiet the mind down long enough to focus its attention on anything. So, while meditation is a good answer, this is exactly what they struggle to do. And which, to begin with, may be why they seek therapeutic relief for their symptoms. I wonder if following the rubric of *asana* and *pranayama* through a practice of movement and music, it may be possible to meet the client where they are in their physical state of agitation. Once there is some synchrony between their agitated body and its expression in movement, it may be possible for them to settle their internal energies and work towards a balanced focus. While meditation may not always correspond with an immersive state, perhaps an emerging state of calm, and balanced harmony within the body will alleviate symptoms of distress and agitation.

Using the framework of *ashta anga yoga* may provide a healer with multiple tools and techniques to work with an individual with a goal to move towards meditative immersion (*dhyana*), where healing may be an autonomous outcome. Such a healing tradition can integrate Western psychotherapeutic interventions with *Bharatha Natyam*, based on *ashta anga* principles. For instance—cognitive, behavioral, existential and person centered therapeutic modalities can work on developing a Yogic life outlook, that includes values of authentic living, empowered interactions, healthy boundaries in relationships, intellectual curiosity, and acceptance of life events. This attitudinal disposition is consistent with yama and niyama aspects of *ashta anga yoga*. I wonder if Western psychotherapeutic interventions emphasize cognitive and behavioral modifications that are conducive to creating change in an individual, and focus less on physical practices that may augment such changes.

As a psychotherapist I am drawn to including individual and group practices that facilitate such change through the physical body. For instance, in working with individuals who have symptoms of thought disorders such as schizophrenia I find that it is especially advantageous to work with their physical body towards creating an internal balance. Using rhythm and movement to create inner flow of energy may hold tremendous potential in correcting inner imbalance that may also manifest as symptoms of identifiable mental disorders. While individual practice is recommended, being a participative observer may also have significant therapeutic outcomes. Intentional community practice of *natya yoga* may have healing outcomes in dancer and audience. This exploration of creative healing approaches that integrate Western psychotherapy with Eastern arts is an area that holds promise for improved efficacy in treating mental illness.

While day-to-day living may challenge an integrated existence, the body's natural tendency may be to re-unite what has become separated, facilitated by practices consistent with principles of *ashta anga yoga*. This study suggests that *Bharatha Natyam* among other practices of *ashta anga yoga* reclaims a natural integration, rejuvenates, and restores vitality to both the practice and practitioner. This study suggests that *Bharatha Natyam* when practiced as *Natya Yoga* heals and transforms the dancer/healer and the participant/observer.

REFERENCES

Ajaya, S. (Ed.) (1980). *Living with the Himalayan Masters: Spiritual experiences of Swami Rama*. Honesdale, PA: Himalayan International Institute of Yoga Science and Philosophy of the USA.

Apffel-Marglin, F. (1985). *Wives of the god-king: The rituals of the devadasis of Puri*. New York, NY: Oxford University Press.

Appa-Rao, P. S. R., & Rama-Sastry, P. (1967). *A monograph on Bharatha's Natya Sastra—Indian dramatology*. Hyderabad, India: Naatya Maala.

Arya, U. (1986). *Yoga-Sutras of Patanjali with the exposition of Vyasa*. Honesdale, PA: Himalayan International Institute of the Science and Philosophy of the USA.

Avalon, A. (1974). *The serpent power: Secrets of Tantric and Shakti yoga*. New York: NY: Dover.

Ballentine, R. M. (1986) Meditation and the unconscious mind. In R. M. Ballentine (Ed.), *The theory and practice of meditation* (Chapter 6). Honesdale, PA: Himalayan International Institute of Yoga Science and Philosophy of the USA.

Barone, T., & Eisner, E. (2012). *Arts Based Research*. Thousands Oaks, CA: Sage.

Berendt, J. (1983). *The world is sound—Nada Brahma: Music and the landscape of consciousness*. Rochester, VT: Destiny Books/Bear & Inner Traditions.

Bharati, S. V. (2001). *Yogasutras of Patanjali with the exposition of Vyasa*. Delhi, India: Motilal Banarsidass.

Bhat, G. K. (1975). *Bharatha Natya Manjari—Bharatha on the theory and practice of drama*. Poona, India: Bhandarkar Oriental Research Institute.

Bloomfield, H. H., Cain, M. P., & Jaffe, D. T. (1975). *TM*: Discovering inner energy and overcoming stress*. New York, NY: Delacorte Press.

Bose, M. (2007). *Movement and mimesis: The idea of dance in the Sanskritic tradition*. New Delhi, India: D.K. Printworld.

Braud, W. (1998). Integral inquiry: Complimentary ways of knowing, being, and expression. In W. Braud & R. Anderson (Eds.), *Transpersonal research methods for the social sciences: Honoring human experience* (pp. 35–68). Thousands Oaks, CA: Sage.

Burley, M. (2000). *Hata Yoga: Its context, theory, and practice*. Delhi, India: Motilal Banarsidass.

Chace, M., Lohn, A., Chaiklin, S., & Sandel, S. L. (1993). *Foundations of dance/movement therapy: The life and work of Marian Chace*. Columbia, MD: Marian Chace Memorial Fund of the American Dance Therapy Association.

Chakravarthi, S. C. (1974). *Samadhi and beyond*. Bedford, MA: CSA Printing and Binding.

Chaudhuri, H. (1965). *Integral yoga: The concept of harmonious and creative living.* London, England: George Allen & Unwin.

Coomaraswamy, A. K. (1985). *The dance of Siva: Essays on Indian art and culture.* New York, NY: Dove.

Coomaraswamy, A. K., & Duggirala, G. K. (1987). *The mirror of gesture—Being the Abhinaya Darpana of Nandikesvara.* New Delhi, India: Munshiram Manoharlal.

Daumal, R. (1982). *Rasa or knowledge of self.* New York, NY: New Directions Books.

Delauriers, D. (1992). Dimensions of knowing: Narrative, paradigm, and ritual. *ReVision, 14*(4), 187–193.

De Marquette, J. (1965). *Introduction to comparative mysticism.* Bombay, India: Bharatiya Vidya Bhavan.

Deshpande, G. T. (1989). *Abhinavagupta.* New Delhi, India: Sahitya Akademi.

Devanand, G. K. (2008). *Teaching of Yoga.* New Delhi, India: APH.

Dey, S. C. (1990). *The quest for music divine.* New Delhi, India: Ashish.

Dhananjayan, V. P. (1984). *A dancer on dance.* Madras, India: Bharatha Kalanjali.

Digambarji, S. (1975). Some thoughts about a few concepts in yoga. In S. Digambarji (Ed.), *Collected papers on yoga* (pp. 29–31). Lonavla, India: Kaivalyadhama.

Digambarji, S., Jha, P., & Sahay, G.S . (Eds. & comm.). (1984). *Vasishta Samhita* (Yoga Kanda). Lonavla [Poona], India: Kaivalyadhama.

Diwakar, R. R. (1975). Yoga: The science and art of conscious human evolution. In S. Digambarji (Ed.), *Collected papers on yoga* (pp. 7–13). Lonavla [Poona], India: Kaivalyadhama.

Eckartsberg, R. V. (1983). Existential-phenomenology, validity, and the transpersonal ground of psychological theorizing. In A. Georgi, A. Barton, & C. Maes (Eds.), *Duquesne studies in phenomenological psychology* (Vol. IV) [pp. 199–206]. Pittsburgh, PA: Duquesne University Press.

Feuerstein, G. (1989). *The Yoga-Sutra of Patanjali: A new translation and commentary*. Rochester, VT: Inner Traditions International.

Feuerstein, G. (1998). *The yoga tradition: Its history, literature, philosophy, and practice*. Prescott, AZ: Hohm Press.

Feuerstein, G. (2003). *The deeper dimension of yoga: Theory and practice*. Boston, MA: Shambhala.

Finger, A., & Repka. K. (2005). *Chakra yoga: Balancing energy for physical, spiritual, and mental well-being*. Boston, MA: Shambala.

Gaston, A. (1982). *Siva in dance, myth, and iconography*. New York, NY: Oxford University Press.

Gautam, M. R. (1993). *Evolution of raga and tala in Indian music*. New Delhi, India: Munshiram Manoharlal.

Ghosh,M. (1967). *The Natyasastra: A treatise on ancient Indian dramaturgy and histrionics ascribed to Bharatha-Muni*. Calcutta, India: Granthalaya.

Ghosh, M. (1981). *Nandikesvara Abhinayadarpanam*. Calcutta, India: Manisha Granthalaya.

Giorgi, A. (Ed.) (1985). *Phenomenology and psychological research*. Pittsburgh, PA: Duquesne University Press.

Gnoli, R. (1968). *The aesthetic experience according to Abhinavagupta*. Varanasi, India: Chowkhamba Sanskrit Series Office.

Goswami, S. (1999). *Layayoga: The definitive guide to the chakras and kundalini*. Rochester, VT: Inner Traditions.

Halprin, A. (2000). *Dance as a healing art: Returning to health through movement and imagery*. Mendocino, CA: LifeRhythm.

Ishvara (2002). *Oneness in living: Kundalini yoga, the spiritual path, and the intentional community*. Berkeley, CA: Northern Atlantic Books.

Iyengar, B. K. S. (1995). *The tree of yoga*. NOIDA, UP: Harper Collins.

Iyengar, B. K. S. (2008). *Light on the Yogasutras of Patanjali*. NOIDA, UP: Harper Collins.

Kothari, S. (Ed.). (1982). *Bharatha Natyam: Indian classical dance art*. Mumbai, Maharashtra, India: Marg.

Kripalvananda, S. (1977). *The science of meditation*. Retrieved from http://www.naturalmeditation.net on 8/7/11.

Krishnamacharya, E. (1976). *The yoga of Patanjali*. Visakhapatanam, India: Mithila.

Kriyananda,G. (1985). *The spiritual science of kriya yoga*. Chicago, IL: Temple of Kriya Yoga.

Kruger, D. (1983). Psychotherapy research and existential-phenomenological psychology: An exploration. In A. Georgi, A. Barton, & C. Maes (Eds.), *Duquesne studies in phenomenological psychology* (Vol. IV) [pp. 8–32]. Pittsburgh, PA: Duquesne University Press.

Kumar, P. (1998). *Introduction to tantras and their philosophy*. New Delhi, India: Rashtriya Sanskrit Sansthan.

Kumar, P. (Ed.) (2006). *Natyasastra of Bharathamuni: Text, commentary of Abhinava Bharati by Abhinavaguptacarya and English translation by M. M. Ghosh*. Delhi, India: New Bharatiya.

Laverty, S. (2003). Hermeneutic phenomenology and phenomenology: A comparison of historical and methodological considerations. *International Journal of Qualitative Methods, 2*(3), 1–29.

Leavy, P. (2009). *Method meets art: Arts based research practice.* New York, NY: Guilford Press.

Levy, F. J. (Ed.). (1992). *Dance/movement therapy: A healing art.* Reston, VA: National Dance Association/ American Alliance for Health, Physical Education, Recreation, and Dance.

Menen, R. (2004). *The healing power of mudras: The yoga of the hands.* Delhi, India: Pushtak Mahal.

Miller, R. S. (1992). *As above, so below: Paths to spiritual renewal in daily life.* Los Angeles, CA: J. P. Tarcher.

Miller, B. S. (1995). *Yoga—Discipline of Freedom—The Yogasutra attributed to Patanjali.* Berkeley, CA: University of California Press.

Mishra, R. S. (1973). *Yogasutras: The textbook of yoga psychology.* New York, NY, Anchor Press.

Moustakas, C. E. (1990). *Heuristic research: Design, methodology, and applications.* Thousands Oaks, CA: Sage.

Moustakas, C. E. (1994). *Phenomenological research methods.* Thousands Oaks, CA: Sage.

Mruk, C. (1983). Toward a phenomenology of self-esteem. In A. Georgi, A. Barton, & C. Maes (Eds.), *Duquesne studies in phenomenological psychology* (Vol. IV) [pp. 137–149]. Pittsburgh, PA: Duquesne University Press.

Mukherji, P. N. (Trans.). (1981). *Yoga philosophy of Patanjali by Samkhya yogacharya Swami Hariharananda Aranya.* Albany, NY: State University of New York Press.

Muktibodhananda, S. (2000). *Hata yoga pradipika* (Light on hatha yoga: including the original Sanskrit text of the Hatha yoga pradipika with translation in English). Fort Munger, Bihar, India: Yoga Publications Trust.

Narayanan, C. R. (2012). *Yoga's approach to universal balance.* Retrieved from http://www.lifeinyoga.org/App_Downloads/Paper_ICCS2012.pdf on 2/7/12.

Narayanan, C.R. (2011). *Yoga's approach to Sustainable Evolution of the Human Being and Societies.* Retrieved from http://www.lifeinyoga.org/App_Downloads/Paper_USF.pdf on 2/7/12.

Narayanan, C. R. (2009). *Redefining yoga in original terms* (Vol. 1), *Yogasutras of Patanjali and Life in Yoga approach.* Silver Spring, MD: Unpublished manuscript.

Narayanan, K. (1994). *Aspects of Abhinaya.* Madras, India, Alliance.

Nelson, P. L. (2000). Mystical experience and radical deconstruction: Through the ontological looking glass. In T. Hart, P. L. Nelson, & K. Puhakka, K. (Eds.), *Transpersonal knowing: Exploring the horizon of consciousness.* Albany, NY: State University of New York Press.

Nikhilananda, S. (Trans.). (1988). *The Gospel of Ramakrishna* (Abridged). New York, NY: Ramakrishna Vivekananda Center. Pallaro, P. (Ed.). (1999). Authentic movement: Essays by Mary Starks Whitehouse, Janet Adler, and Joan Chodorow. Philadelphia, PA: Jessica Kingsley.

Pande, A. (1997). *Abhinavabharati (Abhinavagupta's Commentary on Bharatha's Natyasastra Chapter XXVIII).* Allahabad, India: Raka Prakasahan.

Pande, S. C. (Ed.). (2009). *The concept of Rasa with special reference to Abhinavagupta.* New Delhi, India: Aryan Books International.

Radha, S. (1980). *Mantras: Words of Power*. Kootenay, BC, Canada: Timeless Books.

Raghavan, V. (1980). *Abhinavagupta and his works*. Varanasi, India: Chaukambha Orientalia.

Rama, S. (1983). *Choosing a path*. Honesdale, PA: Himalayan International Institute of Yoga Science and Philosophy of the USA.

Rama, S. (1986). What is meditation? In Ballentine, R.M. (Ed.), *The theory and practice of meditation*. (pp. 9-31). Honesdale, PA: Himalayan International Institute of Yoga Science and Philosophy of the USA.

Ramacharaka, Y. (1930). *Hata yoga or the yogi philosophy of physical well being*. Chicago, IL: Yogi Publication Society.

Ramakrishna, L. (2005). *Sampradaya Sangita: Classical musical tradition*. Bengaluru, India: Kalpatharu Research Academy.

Rangacharya, A. (1986). *Natyasastra: English translation with critical notes*. Bangalore, India: IBH Prakashana.

Riessman,C. K. (2008). *Narrative methods for the human sciences*. Thousands Oaks, CA: Sage.

Ross, J. (2007). Anna Halprin: Experience as dance. Berkeley, CA: University of California Press.

Sadhu, M. (1962). *Samadhi: The superconsciousness of the future*. London, England: George Allen & Unwin.

Sahai, M. (1975). Yoga concepts corresponding to consciousness. In S. Digambarji (Ed.). *Collected papers on yoga* (pp. 23–27). Lonavla, India: Kaivalyadhama.

Sairam, T. V. (2010). Nada Yoga: The yoga of music. *Bhavans Journal, 57*(3), 72–76.

Satchidananda, S. (1990). *The Yogasutras of Patanjali*. Yogaville, VA: Integral Yoga.

Satchidananda Ashram-Yogaville (Producer). (2002, May 25). Transcending body and mind (DVD). Virginia, United States: Shakticom/Integral Yoga Multimedia. (Available at http://www.shakticom.org/Swami-Satchidananda/DVDs/Essential-Teachings/Q-A-Transcending-Body-and-Mind-DVD/prod_203.html)

Schwandt, T. A. (2007). *The Sage dictionary of qualitative inquiry* (3rd ed.). Thousands Oaks, CA: Sage.

Sela-Smith, S. (2002). Heuristic research: A review and critique of Moustakas' method. *Journal of Humanistic Psychology, 42*(3), 53–88.

Shah, J. B. (Ed.). (2003). *Abhinavabharati text: Restored and other articles* (The collected papers contributed by Prof. V.M. Kulkarni). Ahmedabad, India: Shresthi Kasturbhai Lalbhai Amarek Nidhi.

Shastri, K. (1975). A historical review of yoga. In D. Digambarji (Ed.), *Collected papers on yoga* (pp. 14–23). Lonavla, India: Kaivalyadhama.

Shringy, B. K., & Sharma, P. L. (Trans.). (2007). *Sangitaratnakara of Sarngadeva: Sanskrit text and English translation with comments and notes* (Vol. 1). New Delhi, India: Munshiram Manoharlal.

Shrivastava, G. M. L. (1987). *The yoga of Patanjali and the integral yoga of Sri Aurobindo*. Delhi, India: Vishwa/Kala Prakashan.

Siegel, L. (1978). *Sacred and profane dimensions of love in Indian traditions as exemplified in the Gitagovinda of Jayadeva*. Oxford, UK: Oxford University Press.

Singleton, M. (2010). *Yoga body: The origins of modern posture practice*. New York, NY: Oxford University Press.

Sivananda, S. (1952). *Japa yoga: A comprehensive treatise on mantra shastra*. Rishikesh, India: Yoga-Vedanta Forest University.

Sivananda, S. (1960). *Fourteen lessons in Raja Yoga.* Tehri-Garhwal, U.P., India: Divine Life Society.

Sivananda, S. (1970). *Practice of yoga* (rev. 4th ed.). Tehri-Garhwal, U.P., India: Divine Life Society.

Sovatsky, S. (2009). On being moved: Kundalini and the complete maturation of the spiritual body. In G. K. Khalsa, A. Newberg, S. Rhada, K. Wilber, & J. Selby (Eds.), *Kundalini rising: Exploring the energy of awakening* (pp. 247–268). Louisville, CO: Sounds True.

Subrahmanyam, P. (n.d.). *Some pearls from the fourth chapter of Abhinavabharati.* Retrieved from http://www.svabhinava.org/abhinava/PadmaSubrahmanyam/PadmaSub.pdf on 4/24/11.

Tigunait, R. (1996). *The power of mantra and the mystery of initiation.* Honesdale, PA: Himalayan International Institute of Yoga Science and Philosophy of the USA.

Tirth, S. S. (1997). *A guide to Shaktipat.* New York, NY: Swami Shivom Tirth Ashram.

Vatsyayan, K. (1968). *Classical Indian dance in literature and the arts.* New Delhi, India: Sangeet Natak Akademi.

Vatsyayan, K. (1974). *Indian classical dance.* India: Publications Division, Ministry of Information and Broadcasting, Govt. of India.

Vatsyayan, K. (1996). *Bharatha: The Natyasastra.* New Delhi, India: Sahitya Akademi.

Vivekananda, S. (1998). *Raja yoga or conquering the internal nature.* Advaita Ashrama, Calcutta, India.

Wells, K. (2011). *Narrative inquiry.* New York: Oxford University Press.

Whicher, I. (1998). *The integrity of yoga darsana: A reconsideration of classical yoga.* Albany, NY: State University of New York Press.

Whicher, I., & Carpenter, D. (2003). *Yoga: The Indian tradition.* London, England: Routledge Curzon.

Willcox, l. C. (1914). The Dionysian quality in Victorian poetry. *North American Review, 199*(702), 747–755.

Yardi, M. R. (1979). *The Yoga of Patanjali.* Poona, India: Bhandarkar Oriental Research Institute.

Yogananda, P. (1997). *Journey to self-realization.* Los Angeles, CA: Self-Realization Foundation.

ABOUT THE AUTHOR

Aparna Ramaswamy is a dancer, teacher and psychotherapist whose passion is to help others reclaim their innate ability to heal and overcome emotional distress. With over forty years of training in *Bharatha Natyam*, she believes in the healing power of movement, music & meditation. Aparna holds a Masters degree in Clinical Counseling from Johns Hopkins University and a Ph.D. in Transformative Studies from California Institute of Integral Studies and. She follows an integrative healing model (*Natya yoga* therapy) that combines movement, music and meditation with conventional psychotherapy, a direct outcome of her Ph.D. research and lifetime practice of *natya yoga*.

Aparna has taught *Bharatha Natyam* for over twenty years in the Washington, DC metro area. She is a critically acclaimed dancer & teacher whose students have represented Indian dance at community events, educational institutions and cultural organizations. As Faculty Associate at Johns Hopkins University, she teaches and offers supervision to counselors-in-training in the Masters program in Counseling. Aparna is a published writer of several research studies on efficacy of Natya Yoga therapy in overcoming psychiatric distress and disorders. She offers meditation sessions, counseling services and advanced training in Bharatha Natyam – each practice based on the core principles of *ashta anga yoga*.

Website: www.NatyaYogaTherapy.net

Printed in Great Britain
by Amazon